ILLUSTRATED
MISSION FURNITURE CATALOG
1912-13

COME-PACKT
FURNITURE COMPANY

EDITED BY
VICTOR M. LINOFF

DOVER PUBLICATIONS, INC., NEW YORK

Published in Canada by General Publishing Company, Ltd., 30 Lesmill Road, Don Mills, Toronto, Ontario.
Published in the United Kingdom by Constable and Company, Ltd., 3 The Lanchesters, 162–164 Fulham Palace Road, London W6 9ER.

This Dover edition, first published in 1991, is an unabridged republication of the Come-Packt Furniture Company catalog published in 1912. The Introduction by Victor M. Linoff was specially written for this edition.

Manufactured in the United States of America
Dover Publications, Inc., 31 East 2nd Street, Mineola, N.Y. 11501

Library of Congress Cataloging-in-Publication Data

Come-Packt Furniture Company.
    [Come-Packt Furniture Company catalog]
    Illustrated mission furniture catalog, 1912–13 / Come-Packt Furniture Company ; edited by Victor M. Linoff. — Dover ed.
        p.   cm.
    Unabridged republication of the catalog entitled: Come-Packt Furniture Company catalog, published in 1912.
    ISBN 0-486-26529-3
    1. Come-Packt Furniture Company—Catalogs.   2. Furniture, Mission—Catalogs.   I. Linoff, Victor M.   II. Title.
NK2439.C65A4   1991
684.1′029′477113—dc20   90-45416
                                                                           CIP

INTRODUCTION

"A MAN is judged as much by the furnishings in his home as . . . by the clothes he wears or the friends he cultivates—it does not cost as much to have Come-Packt furniture in your home as the 'near' furniture, and its quality and appearance calls [sic] for no apology." That proud statement (from page 20 of this volume) was one of many used to persuade the American consumer in 1912 of the superiority of Come-Packt Furniture Company goods and the cost savings of its special brand of mail-order shopping.

For the United States, the beginning of the twentieth century was a period of exciting growth. The automobile was rapidly becoming the standard mode of surface transportation. Man's first powered flight into the skies had captured the imagination of the world. The telephone was already common in households and businesses. Rural isolation, as it had been experienced in the nineteenth century and before, was now a part of history. The railway network by now was serving all but the most remote communities. The relative ease with which goods could be shipped meant greater rural accessibility to big-city markets, and allowed the growth of large mail-order houses like Sears, Roebuck and Montgomery Ward. Contentment, prosperity and wonderful dreams of what this new century would offer gave Americans an optimistic outlook in the years before World War I.

As the century began, a rebellion of sorts was taking place against many of the constraints and extravagances of the Victorian era. John Ruskin, Charles Eastlake and William Morris had already helped England lead the way down a new road toward simpler design and decor. In the United States, Gustav Stickley, through his Craftsman Workshop, and Elbert Hubbard's Roycrofters were now picking up the banner and colorfully proclaiming the new philosophy and design aesthetic.

Variously known as Mission, Arts & Crafts, Craftsman and Quaint, this rather stern design, introduced in the United States by Stickley about 1898, was the innovation Americans were looking for. Many were ready and eager to abandon the overly ornate and fussy mode so characteristic of the Victorian era, as became evident in the rapid public acceptance of this new style. The bungalow, a new and allied form of residential architecture, was the perfect setting for the new furnishing style, and for many the combination was irresistible.

All across the United States, from big city to farming hamlet, the Mission movement spread. Stickley's imitators and competitors flooded the market with Mission designs to satisfy an ever-increasing consumer demand. Mail-order companies were offering not only simple, "honest," rectilinear furniture and decorative accessories, but also, in the case of large firms like Sears, Roebuck, the homes appropriate to this rather severe, basic style. Even Stickley's brothers got into the act, founding the firms of L. & J. G. Stickley in Fayetteville, New York, and Stickley Brothers Co. in Grand Rapids.

Such was the scene when the Come-Packt Furniture Company was established in 1907. The firm's name indicated the most salient feature of its extensive line: the furniture would "come packed" in a "compact" parcel. In a time when nearly all long-distance shipments were made by rail, bulk rather than weight was the major cost factor. By producing furniture that could be shipped knocked down, a significant freight savings was effected. (The special design features of the furniture are described in the "Construction Details" on page 4.)

Shipping furniture disassembled was not a new idea; furniture stores usually received their merchandise in this form. What was new was the idea of the consumer doing his own assembly "with the aid of an ordinary screw driver" (p. 2). But even imaginative design could not produce an entire line of sectional furniture. The catalog's first forty-five pages display furniture that could be shipped knocked down; the remainder illustrates pieces that had to be delivered in assembled form.

Since they only marketed direct, Come-Packt's primary mode of communication with its customers was through advertisements in major periodicals. Their ads were frequently seen in the *Saturday Evening Post, Ladies' Home Journal, Everybody's Magazine, Literary Digest* and Elbert Hubbard's *The Fra,* and each ad touted the freight savings of shipping sectional furniture.

The ninth catalog offered by Come-Packt, for 1912-1913, is reproduced here. Only five years after its founding, the company can claim a capital stock as substantial as $100,000. (Consider that the average American wage earner of the time was earning about ten dollars a week.) The catalog illustrates a comprehensive line of more than 400 items—everything from asbestos tabletop pads to window seats—and provides not only a fascinating look at the furniture and accessory styles of the day but also a wealth of secondary information.

The upholstery and finish color chart, for example (see inside back cover), offers the historian and restorer a rare view of the diverse palette and materials appropriate to the Mission style. Valuable details about the resources and techniques used in creating Mission finishes can be found on page 73.

There are descriptions of the various woods used in furniture making, including their strengths and weaknesses. The catalog continually emphasizes the manufacturer's preference for white oak, "which has a beautiful flaky grain, instead of the coarse, *'stringy'* grain of Red Oak" (p. 11). An illustrated description of the difference between plain and quartersawn oak is also provided (p. 7).

Upholstery materials, we learn, could vary from leathers and imitation leathers to mohair, tapestry and even denim.

On page 36 the catalog generously offers advice on the care of furniture, most of which is still valuable today.

Acknowledging that "not everyone admires the pure Mission, or Arts and Crafts lines" (p. 47), the catalog also offers more traditional styles: Flanders, "Colonial" and Virginia Colonial, Classic revival, overstuffed (chairs), Turkish (rockers), Bungalow and even a modest offering of woven willow.

By 1910 the traditional parlor was giving way to a new interior-design conception: the living room. One of the first commercial appearances of that term is in this catalog, and page 8 is headlined "Living Room Furniture." Here once again, Come-Packt heralds its leadership in design and marketing:

> One of the most significant developments of modern home architecture is the Living Room, with its simple, harmonious furnishings.
> The keynote of the Living Room is *comfort*. The furniture should be selected with a view to utility and harmony.
> COME-PACKT Living Room furniture is characterized by that simplicity which is the very essence of good taste and embodies the highest art of the furniture designer.

On page 43, the copywriter offers a passing tribute to their major competitor Elbert Hubbard, attesting to his significance as a philosopher and manufacturer: "The hairy Hubbard of East Aurora [New York] has said: 'We make our living from our friends,' and it's true because our enemies never buy from us."

Along with a diverse line of oak, walnut, mahogany and imitation-mahogany furniture, Come-Packt provides two pages of what is now called "Bar Harbor"-style willow furniture (pp. 57, 58). Its quality is emphasized by the statement that all the Willo-Weave line is handmade from imported material by immigrants trained "in their native land."

The four pages of lamps and ceiling fixtures (pp. 59–62), including gas, oil and electric models, display an interesting adjunct to the Mission furniture line, and point to the importance of total coordination of design and decor elements in the Mission style.

As if to provide something for everyone, Come-Packt also offers Mission pianos and player pianos, lace curtains, sewing machines (in cabinet style—decidedly not Mission), kitchen cabinets and accessories.

A surprising inclusion in the catalog is the listing of C. G. Quackenbush as designer (p. 1). In the early years of industrial production of furniture, design was usually the secondary responsibility of an officer or engineer. Not only is this one of the first commercial catalogs to credit its designer, but, just as significantly, on the same page Come-Packt proclaims itself as "Designers—Manufacturers—Sellers."

More research will be necessary to establish the entire story and chronology of this interesting company. It is yet unclear where they began business. An ad in a 1909 issue of *Everybody's Magazine* uses "Come-Packt" as a trade name, but International Manufacturing Company is listed as manufacturer. No early history of that firm is yet known, either. By 1911 the business name had changed to "Come-Packt Furniture Company" and a Toledo, Ohio, address appears. Does that mean it expanded into another market, or was the Ann Arbor company purchased by Toledo interests? Regardless, it is an indication of the firm's early growth and success that, in only four years, Come-Packt was manufacturing and shipping from two locations. And yet, less than a decade after it was established, the Come-Packt name disappears entirely from furniture-manufacturer trade directories. Was it a casualty of World War I? Had furniture styles and market demand so changed that it was no longer able to compete? Did the increased competition from local outlets finally spell its demise? Or did it merge into another, as yet unknown, company?

In time, we may hope to have the answers to these questions. But for now, while the mystery of Come-Packt lingers, a wonderfully informative record of its output is forever preserved in this marvelous catalog.

Victor M. Linoff

COME-PACKT
FURNITURE COMPANY

Designers   **Manufacturers**   **Sellers**

ANN ARBOR
MICH.

FACTORIES U. S. A.

TOLEDO
OHIO

Officers and Directors
BEN RILEY, *President and General Manager*
FRANK A. STIVERS, *Vice-President*
CHARLES W. GAY, *Secretary*
ADAM SCHAUSS, *Treasurer*
L. D. CARR
H. W. DOUGLAS
ALFRED E. JENNINGS

C. G. QUACKENBUSH, *Designer*

Incorporated 1907
CAPITAL STOCK $100,000.00
Copyright, 1912, by Come-Packt Furniture Co.
Cable Address: "COME-PACKT"

Address all Communications to
the Company at

1650 Fernwood Ave., Toledo, Ohio.

CATALOG "H"

Our Guarantee.—A copy of the following **Guarantee** is packed in each box of furniture shipped by the **Come-Packt Furniture Company**:—

"We Guarantee the goods in this shipment to be of perfect design, workmanship and materials and that they will be found exactly as represented in all of our circulars, advertisements and printed matter. We agree to make good any defect in workmanship or materials within one year from date of purchase at our own expense, and we will cheerfully refund purchase price and freight charges if you are not satisfied with your purchase and that you have value received for your money." Our Guarantee means just what we would like to have it mean if we were buying **Come-Packt** instead of selling it.

Our Prices.—All **Come-Packt prices** are **net** and f. o. b. (packed, free on board cars) Ann Arbor, Mich., or Toledo, O. Prices do **not** include freight charges and we make no discount for quantity. A net extra charge of five percent will be made on all orders boxed for Foreign shipment, except to Canada or Mexico. All Come-Packt Sectional Furniture will be completely assembled and shipped ready for use (except dining tables and bed davenports) for five percent extra to cover cost of assembling and packing. All **sectional furniture** will be shipped **in sections,** but completely stained and finished unless otherwise ordered. A hand rubbed and polished varnish finish, 10 per cent. additional to cost of mission finishes.

Prices in this catalog supersede all previous catalogs (A-B-C-D-E-F-G-12.)

Terms.—Our Terms are cash in advance, or 25 percent when the order is placed and the balance to be collected by draft attached to Bill of Lading. On orders amounting to less than $10.00, cash in full should accompany the order, or collection charges must be assumed by the purchaser.

Our References—We refer you to the Ann Arbor Banks, Second National Bank, Toledo, Ohio or to Dun's Agency as to our responsibility and financial standing. The best Guarantee of our good faith is the fact that we have been continuous advertisers in the best of the National Publications and Magazines ever since the inception of this business in 1907.

Fine Furniture at Very Low Cost

It is the laudable ambition of every home lover to buy furniture that will not only meet all requirements as to utility and convenience but possesses in itself such artistic and intrinsic merit that it lends an added charm to home life.

It is unfortunately true that almost or fully half of the cost of furniture purchased through the regular retail channels does not go into the furniture itself, but is eaten up in the tremendous selling expenses incidental to that system of merchandising.

The inevitable result is that countless homes are filled with nondescript collections of furniture, inferior in quality and entirely lacking in the harmony which should characterize all appointments of the home.

The basic idea behind **Come-Packt Furniture** is to give to the actual user not only the benefit of factory prices and honest values, but a unity in artistic design which it is impossible to secure when purchases are made from miscellaneous stocks of retail dealers which come from different factories and vary widely in design and finish.

Come-Packt Furniture enables you to secure artistic unity and intrinsic value in furniture at about half the outlay which would be necessary in purchasing a miscellaneous assortment of furniture from local stores.

Come-Packt Furniture is Good Furniture

Come-Packt Furniture is good furniture, built with the care and skill of the old-time cabinet makers who loved their craft and wrought out in enduring oak their ideals of utility and beauty.

Modern machinery performs with vastly greater economy and precision many operations which in the olden days were laboriously done by hand, but the key-note of "Come-Packt" design and construction,—"Use made beautiful"—remains the same. It is true to the best ideals of the master craftsman who created the artistic types now reproduced and modernized in "Come-Packt" Furniture.

Built in Sections

We build **Come-Packt** Furniture in finished sections which can be quickly and easily assembled by the purchaser with the aid of an ordinary screw driver.

This unique method of construction has much to do with the extraordinarily low prices which we make. Aside from the saving in labor, which of course is a comparatively small item, it means great economy in packing and shipping, doing away with the necessity for expensive and unwieldy crates and affords the customer a very important saving in freight.

Sectional or "knocked down" furniture takes a lower freight rate, because it only occupies a fraction of the space required in shipping completed furniture.

In addition to the advantages above mentioned, sectional furniture is a guarantee against the use of "dowel" joints in place of the strong and perfect fitting "mortise" and "tenon" joints, which you will find used in Come-Packt Sectional Furniture.

It is an easy matter for the furniture manufacturer to cover up cheap, flimsy construction, giving it the outward appearance of stability and strength, which it does **not** possess.

The Growing Popularity of Come-Packt Furniture

Come-Packt Furniture has been on the market for years and has steadily grown in public favor as its wonderful economy, its artistic excellence and inherent quality have become known to an ever widening circle of home lovers.

While in our advertising we have always given great emphasis to the low prices at which it is sold, the dominating thought of its makers has from the very first been **quality.**

We always welcome trial orders for individual pieces of Come-Packt Furniture, not because of the profit we make on a single piece, for such profit is a mere trifle.

The first piece of Come-Packt Furniture that enters the home affords proof positive that all our claims and promises as to quality, satisfaction and service are fulfilled in ample measure. In the vast majority of cases, it is followed by additional orders, for those who once learn what surprising values we give are never satisfied until their homes are completely and harmoniously furnished with Come-Packt Furniture.

The Come-Packt Line is Complete

You will find in this catalog accurate illustrations and detailed descriptions of the entire **Come-Packt** line of furniture for every room in the house. Furniture of distinguished beauty, harmonious in design. Furniture

that will create an impression of good taste and refinement among your friends. Furniture that will endure through generations.

There are hundreds of beautiful Mission, Flanders and Colonial designs in Quarter-Sawn White Oak,—Period Furniture in Solid Mahogany, luxuriously upholstered rockers, chairs and davenports in a variety of coverings; handsome rugs, curtains, willow furniture and lighting fixtures.

Among the most splendid examples of **Come-Packt** craftsmanship are the magnificent pianos and player pianos.

Each separate piece of Come-Packt Furniture is covered by our broad and binding guarantee; the strongest that can be devised for the safeguarding of the purchaser.

Come-Packt Prices Save You 25 to 50 Per Cent.

Our prices on Come-Packt Guaranteed Furniture save the purchaser an average of 25 to 50 per cent. This is a real, bona-fide and unquestioned saving. The most careful comparison as to quality and value will prove it to your entire satisfaction. Many thousands of the most critical and careful judges of furniture have proved to themselves that "Come-Packt" is far above the average in quality and 50 per cent below the prevailing prices of retail stores.

But we do not base our appeal for your patronage solely upon the extraordinarily low prices we offer. Price is not the criterion of **value.**

There are other considerations more important than its price that should influence your decision in favor of **Come-Packt** Furniture.

We offer you furniture that will give lasting satisfaction for many years to come, because it possesses **character** and **quality,** beauty of **line,** harmony in **design,** individuality and an artistic charm all its own.

We Are Manufacturers—Not Mere Mail-Order "Distributors"

Do not confuse this company with concerns selling furniture by mail, who merely distribute the products of various outside factories. We are **manufacturers** of **Come-Packt Furniture** with big, well equipped factories in Toledo, Ohio, and Ann Arbor, Michigan.

We **specialize** on fine furniture and center upon its production all our resources, experience and skill. We have established a **standard** of **quality** which is guaranteed by the **"Come-Packt"** Trade Mark, branded on all our furniture. Come-Packt Furniture has won a reputation for quality and value which **we,** as manufacturers, must rigidly maintain.

We have developed the building of furniture into an art. We have gathered about us a peerless organization of artists and craftsmen who give to the making of Come-Packt Furniture the very best that's in them.

Harmonious Rooms

Good taste demands that a room, whether simply or elaborately furnished, shall be free from the discordant and unpleasant effect of ill matched furniture.

Mahogany "quarrels" with Oak and extreme contrasts in design or finish of various articles of furniture in the same room should be avoided.

Simplicity is preferable to over-ornamentation. It costs no more to secure harmonious results in home furnishings, but it does require taste and good judgment to choose furniture that will give permanent satisfaction.

The convenient grouping of the different styles of Come-Packt Furniture in this catalog makes it easy to select furniture that harmonizes in every particular.

Our customers often call on us to suggest the most desirable combinations for various rooms, supplying us with drawings showing the size and arrangement of the rooms to be furnished. We are always glad to render such service without charge and even to suggest color schemes for interior decorations so that the customer may secure the best possible setting for **Come-Packt** Furniture.

Our Pledge to You

This may be the first time you have ever seriously considered the question of purchasing Come-Packt Furniture.

When you compare our prices with the prices you have been accustomed to paying, it may be hard for you to understand how it is possible for us to give such remarkable values.

Or you may not be accustomed to purchasing by mail and feel that you run some risk in buying direct from the factory on the **Come-Packt** plan.

We take this opportunity to state with all possible emphasis that all of our claims are strictly true,—that the equal of Come-Packt Furniture cannot be secured from retail stores at anywhere near our low prices,—that your order by mail is absolutely safeguarded by our guarantee and that we shall spare no effort to serve you.

May we not have the pleasure of adding **your name** to our long list of satisfied customers?

Our Selling Plan

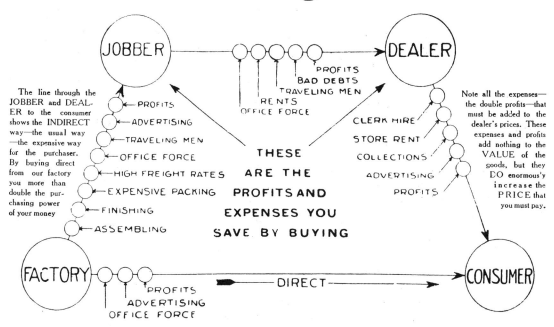

OUR SELLING PLAN—Sectional Furniture, direct from Factory to User, means ECONOMY in manufacturing, selling, shipping and finishing. Our whole effort is directed towards producing and marketing the highest grade of furniture for the least money. The continuous patronage of our customers is the life blood of our business. We aim to conduct our business so that every purchaser becomes a permanent customer and an effective and willing advertiser of our goods. Study the diagram and our selling plan above.

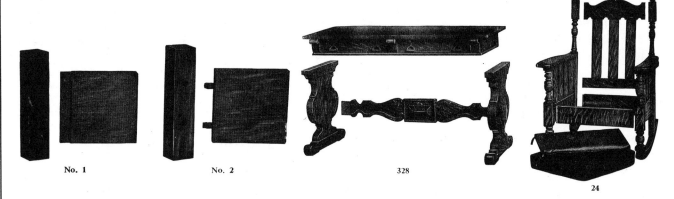

No. 1   No. 2   328   24

Construction Details

In the greater number of our designs, the sections are put together with screws, or patent fasteners. There is no sanding, fitting or other tool work for you to do before putting the sections together. When the sections are together, the furniture is substantial, solid, durable, and except in a very few cases cannot be taken apart for re-shipment.

Illustration No. 328 shows the sections of one of our Library Tables, one of the handsomest of our tables, and an easy one to assemble.

No. 24 shows the sections of one of our rockers. These two pieces, selected at random, show the ease and simplicity of putting the assembled sections together. No skill or mechanical knowledge is necessary—a few minutes work will assemble our largest pieces. The life of a piece of furniture depends, first, on the materials used, and second, on the way the different pieces or parts are put together.

Whenever a joint is to be made that from its nature cannot be satisfactorily held together with patent fasteners or screws, we use the "Mortise and Tenon" joint (see illustration No. 1), and make the tenons the full width of the materials used and at least ¾ of an inch long—this gives ample surface for holding the glue; we know that these joints cannot shrink and work loose after hard service—they cost considerably more to make than the "dowel" joint (see illustration No. 2), but they are well worth the extra cost in the satisfaction of knowing we have not "skimped" in our construction details.

Note the small surface afforded by the "dowel" joint, which has only the strength of the pins shown, yet the dowel joint is used in nine-tenths of the furniture made by other manufacturers.

Until furniture has been used for a year or more, you may not appreciate just what it means to the life of the piece to have not only the best materials used, but to have all joints perfectly made and of sufficient strength to stand constant and hard service, and possibly some abuse, without necessitating a trip to the furniture hospital.

Whenever necessary, we send liquid glue to spread on the tenons before inserting them in the mortises—we use the best quality of glue and know that the joint will be perfect and give lasting satisfaction to the user. In all other parts of the construction, we use just as great care as in making the mortise and tenon joints.

The best French Bevel Plate Mirrors are used exclusively, except in Dressing Tables, where Plain Triplicate Mirrors are necessary.

Where it is structurally possible to use a solid top, we furnish the best Solid Quarter Sawn White Oak top that is specially matched up for figure and grain. On a few tables, on account of their construction, we have found it advisable to make use of a five-ply laminated top. They are the best that can be procured and show beautifully figured tops. We guarantee them to be permanently satisfactory or will replace them at our own expense.

READ BEFORE ORDERING

When Ordering—Give the *Catalog Number* of each piece and *state the color* of *stain, cushions, etc., desired*; also specify whether furniture is to be "stained" or "in the white", also specify how much money is enclosed and in what form—post office money order, which you secure at the postoffice; express money order, which you secure at the express office; bank draft, which you secure at your bank, or send us personal check. We recommend the Postoffice and Express orders as being perhaps, the safest and most convenient way to send money. Always register a letter that contains currency or stamps. Our order sheet is a convenience—not a necessity. Write all in a letter if you prefer.

New Designs—We originate our own designs and all furniture listed by us is made in our own factories. In designing a piece we keep in mind several points—it must have refinement of outline, utility, durability and correct proportions. The sectional furniture must be so designed that it can be put together easily and without the aid of clamps, wedges and the usual cabinet-makers' tools. The assembling of the sections must be so simple that it will be IMPOSSIBLE for a person to put the sections together in any way but the right way. Nothing is left to guess work. We will send you cuts of new designs as we get them out.

Special Work—We do not do special work, or make alterations in our regular designs. We receive so many requests for special cushions, special designs in furniture, or requests for alterations of designs or dimensions that we find it necessary to particularly emphasize that we cannot make any exceptions to this rule.

How Goods are Shipped—Shipping by freight is usually the cheapest way to forward goods weighing over twenty pounds. The railroads have what is called a "minimum charge," which means the least amount of money they will haul a shipment for, no matter how little it weighs. The minimum charge is usually figured on the basis of one hundred pounds at either the first or second class rate. It is on the account of the minimum charge that we recommend that your order be for one or more pieces weighing over 100 pounds. All shipments weighing over 100 pounds are charged for at actual weight. *See table of freight rates on last page.*

Shipments by freight are safe and reliable, and the freight never amounts to much compared with the saving you make on every purchase. Remember that the Dealer has to pay freight on the completed furniture and the freight charges are always added to his selling prices.

The freight agent at your station will notify you when goods arrive and the freight charges are paid when you take the goods from the station. There is no difference in rates whether freight is paid here or at destination.

Prepaying Freight Charges—We do not prepay freight charges on our furniture for the reason that where a delivered price is made, the freight charges are always added to the selling price, and our prices would have to be raised to cover the freight charges all over the United States.

If there is no freight agent at your station, enclose enough money to prepay freight charges, or we will send the goods to the nearest station where there is an agent. (Send too much money rather than too little. We will immediately refund the difference).

Prompt Shipments—We aim to keep a large stock on hand at all times and make immediate shipment of all orders coming to us as soon as they can be finished and packed.

Time Allowance for Finishing Furniture—All furniture (except Mahogany, Birch Mahogany and white enamel pieces), are kept in stock "in the white" (unfinished) and for a Mission finish you should allow not less than four days to six for the finishing process as a good durable finish cannot be put on in less time.

Any Oak piece will be given a hand rubbed varnish finish at a net extra cost of ten per cent. Allow not less than fifteen days for a hand rubbed varnish, or bright varnish finish as a good finish cannot be put on in less time. We take pride in our finishes and do not like to hurry this part of the work. Genuine Mahogany, Birch Mahogany and white enamel pieces are kept in stock completely finished and ready to ship as soon as cushions are made up for upholstered pieces, (your choice of bright or dull finish, specify when ordering or the dull finish will be sent).

Delayed Shipments—If, for any reason we cannot make shipment of your order immediately, we will notify you to this effect, and either ship when the goods are ready to go forward or refund the money in full.

Tracing Shipments—Wait a reasonable length of time before requesting our Traffic Department to trace a shipment; give the goods time to reach destination. However, if a shipment is unreasonably delayed, we will spare no effort to trace the shipment for you and will consider it a favor to have you call on us for all assistance necessary.

Damaged Goods—It is very seldom that goods packed by us reach destination in damaged condition; but if they are damaged, in any way, see that the Freight Agent makes a notation on the freight bill that you pay, stating what the damage consists of, and you then have the basis for a claim for damages. Unless these facts are plainly written across the face of the freight receipt, you cannot enter a claim for damage or shortage. We will not be responsible for glass, or other parts, broken or damaged while in transit, unless the paid freight bill is sent to us with the Agent's notation showing the nature of the damage, or if this cannot be obtained, an affidavit sworn to before a Notary, as to the nature of the damage, will be accepted in its stead, both by us and the Railroad Companies when filing a claim.

When speaking of the sides of a chair, rocker, etc., always state "right" or "left" side as sitting in chair: Other pieces are either "right" or "left" as you face the front of the piece.

City Delivery—May be simplified by mentioning in your order the name of some local cartage, drayage or transfer company. We will then ship to you in care of that company and they will deliver the furniture immediately upon arrival and collect from you for freight charge (if not prepaid), and their small charge for cartage from the depot to your home.

Goods to be Returned—We will give full shipping instructions on all goods that are to be returned to us for any reason whatsoever. DO NOT RETURN GOODS WITHOUT FIRST COMMUNICATING WITH US, as we can frequently adjust matters satisfactory to you without the delay of returning them. Always see that your name and address are plainly written or stamped on packages which are to be returned to us.

Claims—Our Claim Department will, if desired, enter all claims for lost or damaged goods, when the freight receipt (expense bill) is returned to us with proper notation on same, showing the goods to have been damaged in transit. All money paid on claims will be immediately returned to you.

Sectional Furniture—The fore part of this catalog is given over to our sectional furniture. All pieces are kept "in the white" until ordered. Allow sufficient time for finishing when placing your order. Unless otherwise mentioned in the description of the piece, all Sectional Furniture is made of Quarter Sawn White Oak and every process from the selection of the rough lumber until the goods are ready to ship out is watched carefully to insure that every piece shall be worthy of the reputation for quality that has made our Come-Packt Trade Mark so famous wherever furniture is mentioned.

Completed Furniture—To meet the demand for furniture that will be ready as soon as it reaches the home, we have brought out some beautiful designs in White Oak, Genuine Mahogany, Birch Mahogany. Better furniture, or more honestly built furniture is not made. The prices are remarkably low for the quality offered. No attempt has been made to produce cheap goods, but we do make every article as good as it can be made and then sell it as low as it can be consistently marketed for. Our Trade Mark and our Reputation as manufacturers of high class goods is behind every sale. **You must be satisfied.**

Classified Index

Article	Page No.	Article	Page No.	Article	Page No.
Asbestos Pads	71	Dressers	22, 41, 42, 43, 44, 44, 45, 46	Prepaying Freight	5, 72
Beds	41, 43, 44, 45, 46	Dresser Chairs	44, 45, 46	Reception Chairs	22, 23
Bed Davenports	17, 18, 19	Duty Charges	72	References	1
Bed Room Chairs	41	Export Shipments	1, 72	Returned Goods	5
Bed Room Rockers	41	Finishing Materials	71	Rockers 8, 9, 10, 11, 13, 14, 47, 48, 49, 50, 51,	
Book Cases	23, 24, 25	Foot Stools	21	53, 54.	
Book Shelves	23	Freight Rates	5, 72	Screens	22
Buffets	32, 33, 34, 35, 36, 37, 38, 39	Guarantee	1	Sectional Book Cases	25
Casters, (Gliding)	71	Hall Furniture	20	Selling Plan	4
Cellarettes	22	Highboys	42, 43, 44, 45, 46	Settees	13, 14, 49, 50, 51
Chairs	8, 9, 10, 11, 13, 14, 15, 16, 49, 50, 51	Index	6	Serving Tables	32, 35, 36, 37, 38, 39, 40
Cheval Mirrors	41, 42	Kitchen Cabinets	67	Serving Trays	33, 34
Chifforobes	22	Lighting Fixtures	59, 60, 61, 62	Sewing Machines	65, 66
China Closets	32, 33, 35, 36, 37, 38, 39, 40	Library Tables	22, 26, 27, 28, 29	Shirt Waist Boxes	44
Claims	5	Materials	7	Slipper Chairs	41
Clocks	21	Mattresses	68	Special Cushions	70
Construction Details	4	Morris Chairs	12	Special Work	5
Couches	15, 16, 51	Music Cabinets	22	Springs	69
Couch Hammocks	70	New Designs	5	Spring Cushions	7
Curtains	63, 64	Nursery Rockers	22	Sundries	71
Cushions	7, 70	Palm Stands	21, 23	Stains	71, 73, 74
Cushion Materials	7, 73	Paper Baskets	23	Tea Tables	37
Davenports	13, 15, 16, 17, 18, 19, 55, 56	Pedestals	23	Table Covers	70
Desks, (Ladies)	24, 26	Pianos	30, 31	Terms	1
Desks, (Office)	26	Piano Benches	23, 30	Tracing Shipments	5
Desk Chairs	24, 26	Phone Stands	26	Wash Stands	43, 44
Dining Tables	32, 33, 34, 35, 36, 37, 38, 39, 40	Porch Swings	21	Willow Furniture	57, 58
Dining Chairs	32, 33, 34, 35, 36, 38, 39, 40	Prices	1	Window Seats	21

Index of Catalog Numbers with Page Numbers on which They Will Be Found

Cat. No.	Page.	Cat. No.	Page	Cat. No.	Page	Cat. No.	Page	Cat. No.	Page	Cat. No.	Page	Cat. No.	Page
1	12	64	10	212	16	357	24	437	23	622	44	4001	67
2	12	65	10	215	16	358	24	438	21	623	44	to	
3	11	66	10	216	16	359	26	440	22	624	44	4004	67
4	8	67	10	217	14	360	40	442	30	625	22	4201	65
5	8	68	10	218	14	361	40	444	40	627	43	to	
6	9	69	10	219	14	362	40	447	26	628	41	4206	66
7	9	70	9	220	14	364	38	448	40	629	41	4325	70
9	11	71	9	221	14	365	34	450	24	631	42	4326	70
12	41	72	9	222	14	366	26	451	25	632	42	4351	68
13	11	73	9	223	15	367	29	452	25	634	46	to	
14	10	74	13	224	15	369	36	453	23	635	46	4378	69
15	12	75	13	225	17	370	37	454	25	636	46	4401	18
16	12	100	35	231	17	371	33	455	24	637	46	to	
18	9	105	39	241	17	372	32	456	25	638	45	4425	19
22	11	106	39	300	27	373	29	457	38	639	45	4501	53
24	11	109	39	301	28	374	26	458	38	640	45	to	
29	15	110	39	305	28	375	26	459	38	641	45	4508	54
30	13	112	35	309	29	376	27	460	37	642	43	4601	50
31	41	114	40	311	29	377	27	461	37	643	41	to	
32	24-44	115	40	312	22	378	27	462	36	644	43	4623	52
34	10	116	40	317	32	379	24	463	36	645	43	4701	47
35	10	117	40	318	37	380	24	464	34	646	41	to	
40	12	118	36	321	24	385	35	465	33	647	43	4713	48
41	22	119	38	325	39	400	32	466	37	648	46	4801	47
42	22	120	34	326	39	403	23	467	33	660	42	to	
43	21	121	33	327	39	404	23	408	32	666	22	4815	49
44	23	122	33	328	28	408	22	469	36	681	44	4901	59
49	8	123	34	329	29	409	21	470	32	700	20	to	
50	8	124	32	332	24	413	35	471	32	703	20	4928	62
51	8	125	32	333	28	416	23	473	00	704	20	5001	55
52	8	126	36	344	34	417	21	474	23	705	20	to	
53	8	200	13	346	35	418	21	475	23	706	20	5008	56
54	8	201	13	347	29	419	25	503	21	707	20	5101	51
55	9	202	13	348	28	421	39	504	21	708	20	to	
56	9	203	15	349	28	422	39	506	21	709	20	5103	51
57	46	204	14	350	27	427	35	602	15	710	20	5201	57
58	12	205	14	351	27	428	35	604	42	711	21	to	
59	45	206	14	352	28	429	35	610	42	720	20	5218	58
60	26	207	15	353	28	432	21	614	42	721	20	Curtains	
61	26	208	16	354	28	433	34	619	41	1101	25	100	63
62	23	210	16	355	29	434	33	620	44	2020	21	to	
63	23	211	16	356	26	435	22	621	44	2025	21	611	64

Auto Spring Cushions

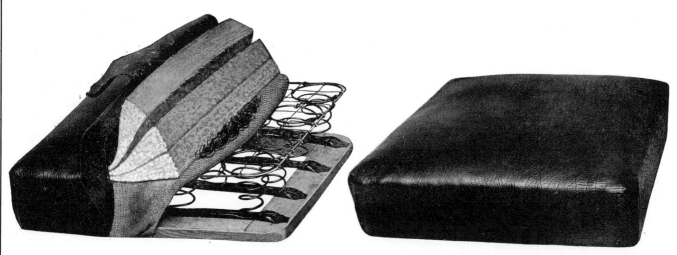

Illustration No. 1

Illustration No. 2

The greatest single advance in modern upholstering is shown above in the two illustrations of our new AUTO-TYPE FLOATING SPRING CUSHION.

Illustration "No. 2" shows the new *Auto-Spring Cushion,* (used in all upholstered COME-PACKT SECTIONAL FURNITURE at the prices shown in this catalog after date of Aug. 1, 1912,) as it appears ready to place in the chair frame. This spring differs greatly from all other spring cushions ever offered with Come-Packt Furniture. It has a spring edge as shown in Illustration No. 1 which allows great freedom of movement and comfort. The cushion is "springy" all over and our construction prevents the sagging of the cushion in the middle as is common with a great many other chairs after they have been in use a short time.

In illustration No. 1 the cover has been partly removed and the spring fabric is shown fastened to a wood frame. The springs are first covered with a well made jacket of burlap, then Moss is built up in the center of the cushion to give the surface a slight oval and further to give the center of the cushion a resiliency that cannot be gained by the use of the cotton felt alone,—then several layers of

pure cotton felt are laid over the Moss and Burlap, bringing the layers well down over the edges of the springs and then the outer casing or cover is put on and the loose edges tacked to the wood base or frame work. A cloth backing is then fastened over the bottom of the frame, making a finished appearance and preventing dust from entering the steel frame work as is the case where open bottom cushions are used.

These cushions are comfortable,—luxuriously so,—they are cool, clean, easily removed and far more responsive and resilient than any other type of floating spring cushion, and we believe this cushion to be the best that has ever been offered at any price.

Auto-Spring Cushions will be furnished on all Sectional chairs, rockers, settees and davenports ordered from this catalog, unless you plainly specify "pillow cushions". All settees and davenport cushions will be furnished in one part instead of two or three as shown. The illustrations in this catalog were taken before we had perfected this Auto Type Spring Cushion and therefore the illustrations do not show how greatly these new cushions add to the attractive appearance of the different designs.

Plain and Quarter Sawn Oak

 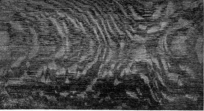 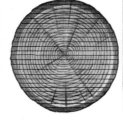 

No. 3

No. 4

No. 5

No. 6

Of near three score varieties of Oak,—WHITE OAK is acknowledged to be the best for fine cabinet work,—it is the hardest, finest textured and best figured, and is capable of taking the finest finish.

We show in the illustrations above just why quartered oak is more expensive to manufacture that the plain sawn oak. The illustration "No. 5" shows the end of a log as it is sawn to produce the plain sawn figure as shown in illustration "No. 6".

Illustration "No. 3" shows the log as it is first sawn into quarters and then each quarter is bisected from the heart to the

bark. Boards are then sawn off parallel to this bisecting section. The medullary rays, or veins running from the heart to the bark are cut and the beautiful figure results as shown in illustration "No. 4". It is these hard flinty medullary rays that give the white oak its amazing strength, and the beautiful irregular markings or flakes. This method of quartering the logs necessitates four times as much handling and entails considerable loss in the material and it makes quartered white oak the most expensive but at the same time the most beautiful native cabinet wood obtainable.

Living Room Furniture

One of the most significant developments of modern home architecture is the Living Room, with its simple, harmonious furnishings.

The keynote of the Living Room is **comfort**. The furniture should be selected with a view to utility and harmony.

COME-PACKT Living Room furniture is characterized by that simplicity which is the very essence of good taste and embodies the highest art of the furniture designer.

You cannot go wrong on making your selections from the many fine pieces of Living Room furniture shown in this catalog.

NOTE—The photographs in this catalog were taken before we had perfected our new auto spring cushion and the cuts therefore do not show the attractive appearance of the new type of cushion. Settee and Davenport cushions will be made in one part instead of two and three as shown.

H4 Rocker

Come-Packt Price $8.45. (Imperial Leather Auto-Spring Cushion). Dealer's price $12.50. Cowhide Covers $10.95. Roan skin $10.15. Dimensions same as H5 Arm Chair. Shipping weight 100 pounds.

H5 Arm Chair

Come-Packt Price $7.75. (Imperial Leather Auto-Spring Cushion.) Dealer's price $12.00. Cowhide Covers, $10.35. Roan skin, $9.45. Height 39 inches. Width 27 inches. Seat 19x19 inches. Legs 1⅝ inches square. Shipping weight 100 pounds.

H53 Chair

H54 Rocker.

Two splendidly designed chairs in quartered oak that will be serviceable as well as ornamental. The rocker is well balanced and is an easy comfortable chair for any occasion. Height 38 inches. Width 28 inches. Shipping weight 80 pounds. Auto-Spring cushions. Dealer's price $14.50.

COME-PACKT PRICE	Imperial Leather	Cowhide	Roan Skin
H54 Rocker	$9.60	$12.40	$11.15
H53 Chair	9.10	11.80	10.60

H49 Arm Chair

Come-Packt Price $9.50. Dealer's price $14.50. (Imperial Leather Auto-Spring Cushion.) Cowhide Covers $11.90. Roan skin $10.95. Height 37 inches. Width 25½ inches. Legs 1 inch flat. Shipping weight 80 pounds.

H52 Chair

H51 Rocker

This chair and its companion the rocker are splendid chairs for the living room, den or office. The posts are 1⅝ inches square and the mortise and tenon construction of all joints insures long life to the chairs even with hard usage.

Quarter Sawn White Oak used exclusively in the construction. Auto-Spring cushions. Height 38 inches. Width 28 inches. Shipping weight 85 pounds. Chairs of equal merit usually retail for $14.00.

COME-PACKT PRICE	Imperial Leather	Cowhide	Roan Skin
H52 Mission Chair	$9.45	$12.25	$10.95
H51 Mission Rocker	9.95	12.80	11.50

H50 Rocker

Come-Packt Price $9.95. Dealer's price $15.00. (Imperial Leather Auto-Spring Cushion.) Cowhide Covers $12.35. Roan skin $11.50. Height 36 inches. Width 25½ inches. Seat 18½ inches. Shipping weight 85 pounds.

QUARTERED SAWN WHITE OAK. A Page of Splendid Values.

H7 Rocker

Come-Packt Price $10.75. (Imperial Leather Auto-Spring Cushions). Retail value $16.50. Cowhide Covers $15.10. Roan skin $14.65. Height 39 inches. Width 29 inches. Seat 19x19 inches. Legs 1⅝ inches square. Shipping weight 90 pounds.

H18coR ker

Come-Packt Price $8.90. Dealer's price $17.00. Imperial Leather Auto-Spring Cushions. Cowhide Covers $13.15. Roan skin $11.40. Height 41 inches. Width 29 inches. Seat 19x19 inches. Legs 1⅝ inches square. Shipping weight 100 pounds.

H6 Arm Chair

Come-Packt Price $10.25. (Imperial Leather Auto-Spring Cushions). Retail value $16.00. Cowhide Covers $14.60. Roan skin $14.15. Height 39 inches. Width 29 inches. Seat 19x19 inches. Shipping weight 90 pounds.

H56 Chair

Come-Packt Price $10.15. (Imperial Leather Auto-Spring Cushions). Retail value $15.75. Cowhide Covers $13.50. Roan skin $12.30. Height 38 inches. Width 28 inches. Seat 19x18 inches. Shipping weight 85 pounds.

H55 Rocker

Come-Packt Price $10.70. (Imperial Leather Auto-Spring Cushions). Retail value $16.25. Cowhide Covers $14.10. Roan skin $12.85. Height 38 inches. Width 28 inches. Seat 19x18 inches. Shipping weight 85 pounds.

H72 Chair

Come-Packt Price $11.25. (Imperial Leather Auto-Spring Cushions). Retail value $18.00. Cowhide Covers $14.00. Roan skin $12.30. Height 42 inches. Width 29 inches. Seat 21½ 21½ inches. Shipping weight 90 pounds.

H71 Rocker

Come-Packt Price $11.55. (Imperial Leather Auto-Spring Cushions). Retail value $18.50. Cowhide Covers $14.30. Roan skin $13.10. Height 39 inches, width 30 inches. Seat 22x21½ in. Posts 2½ in. Shipping weight 100 pounds.

H70 Chair

Come-Packt Price $10.95. (Imperial Leather Auto-Spring Cushions). Retail value $18.00. Cowhide Covers $13.75. Roan skin $12.55. Height 39 inches. Width 30 inches. Seat 22x21½ inches. Shipping weight 100 pounds.

H73 Rocker

Come-Packt Price $11.75. (Imperial Leather Auto-Spring Cushions). Retail value $17.50. Cowhide Covers $14.50. Roan skin $13.30. Height 42 inches. Width 29 inches. Seat 21½x21½ inches. Shipping weight 90 pounds.

Quartered White Oak

H64 Chair

Come-Packt Price $12.45. (Imperial Leather Auto-Spring Cushions). Retail value $20.00. Cowhide Covers $15.75. Roan skin $14.50. Height 36 inches. Width 29 inches. Seat 22x21½ inches. Posts 2½ inches. Shipping weight 100 pounds.

H65 Rocker

Come-Packt Price $12.90. (Imperial Leather Auto-Spring Cushions). Retail value $20.50. Cowhide Covers $16.30. Roan skin $15.10. Height 36 inches. Width 29 inches. Seat 22x21½ inches. Shipping weight 100 pounds.

H14 Rocker

Come-Packt Price $12.40. (Dealer's price $18.50. Imperial Leather Auto-Spring Cushions). Cowhide Covers $15.75. Roan skin $14.65. For Arm Chair to match H14 deduct $0.50 from prices shown. Seat cushions 19x19 inches. Legs 1⅝ inches square. Shipping weight 105 pounds.

H68 Chair

Come-Packt Price $11.55. (Imperial Leather Auto-Spring Cushions). Retail value $19.50. Cowhide Covers $14.30. Roan skin $13.10. Height 36 inches. Width 29 inches. Seat 21½x22 inches. Posts 2½ inches. Shipping weight 100 pounds.

H69 Rocker

Come-Packt Price $12.10. (Imperial Leather Auto-Spring Cushions). Retail value $20.25. Cowhide Covers $14.85. Roan skin $13.60. Height 36 inches. Width 29 inches. Shipping weight 100 pounds.

H34 McKinley Rocker

Come-Packt Price $7.50. Dealer's price $15.00. Imperial Leather Cushions or Cane Seat and Back. Height 32 inches. Width 27½ inches. Seat 20x20 inches. Legs 1½ inches square. Shipping weight 80 pounds.

H66 Chair

Come-Packt Price $12.10. (Imperial Leather Auto-Spring Cushions). Retail value $21.00. Cowhide Covers $15.85. Roan skin $14.60. Height 37 inches. Width 27 inches. Seat 19x20 inches. Posts 2¼ inches. Shipping weight 95 pounds.

H67 Rocker

Come-Packt Price $12.60. (Imperial Leather Auto-Spring Cushions). Retail value $21.50. Cowhide Covers $16.40. Roan skin $15.15. Height 37 inches. Width 27 inches. Seat 19x20 inches. Shipping weight 95 pounds.

H35 McKinley Chair

Come-Packt Price $6.75. Dealer's price $14.25. Imperial Leather Cushions or Cane Seat and Back. Shipping weight 80 pounds.

Beware of "Red Oak" Furniture

The inexperienced furniture buyer should be on guard against the "Red Oak" furniture, which is far inferior in quality to the Quarter Sawed White Oak of which "COME-PACKT" furniture is made. All oak is not Quarter Sawn White Oak any more than all water is pure water.

Comparison of the two classes of oak furniture reveals at a glance the immense superiority of Quarter-Sawed White Oak, which has a beautiful flaky grain, instead of the coarse, "*stringy*" grain of Red Oak.

White Oak is not only more beautifully grained than Red Oak, but because of its firmer texture will take a much finer finish.

H24 Rocker

Come-Packt Price $12.00. (Imperial Leather Auto-Spring Cushion only). Cowhide Covers, $14.90. Roan skin, $13.90. Back cushion complete, Imperial leather, $2.50 extra. Cowhide, $6.50. extra. Roan skin, $5.50 extra. Dealer's price $25.00. Height 41½ inches. Seat 21x22 inches. Shipping weight 110 pounds. Arm Chair to match 50 cents less in price.

PROFIT AND LOSS.

The difference between the first cost and the price you pay is not all profit—some of it is legitimate expense—the cost of doing business. But if you could buy your vegetables from the farmer direct at the price the wholesaler would pay—your coal from the mine in the same way—wool cloth from the mill—hats and trimmings from the manufacturer—couldn't you easily increase the buying power of your money—couldn't you buy more goods for the same money, or get greater value for the price? Look at the diagram of ***our*** selling plan in the fore part of the catalog and see what COME-PACKT means to ***your*** pocketbook.

H22 Rocker

Come-Packt Price $12.75. (With Imperial Auto-Spring Seat Cushion only). Cowhide Covers, $15.65. Roan skin, $14.65. Back cushion complete, Imperial leather $2.50 extra. Cowhide, $6.50. Roan skin, $5.50. Dealer's price $26.75. Height 41½ inches. Seat 21x22 inches. Legs, 2½ inches square. Shipping weight 110 pounds.

H22 Back Cushion

Come-Packt Price (Back cushion only, Imperial leather) $2.50. Cowhide, $6.50. Roan skin, $5.50. Illustration shows the back cushions as applied to H22 and 24. These back cushions are furnished at the extra price shown under the description of each piece. Reversible. Size 16x24 inches.

WHAT ADVERTISING MEANS

Our national advertising campaign does not, in itself, make Come-Packt Furniture better than unadvertised furniture, but it is a bond to you that no misrepresentation will be made of the quality—that you will be protected absolutely by the letter and spirit of our guarantee—that the furniture may be returned at our expense if it is not as represented and satisfactory—and that the goods must be delivered in your home free from accidents due to negligence of the railroads or express companies.

H13 Rocker

Come-Packt Price $12.65. Dealer's price $22.50. Imperial Leather Auto-Spring Cushions. Cowhide Covers $15.50. Roan skin $15.25. Height 42 inches. Seat 21x22 inches. Legs 2½ inches square. Shipping weight 100 pounds.

H3 Rocker

Come-Packt Price $10.45. Dealer's price $19.50. Imperial Leather Auto-Spring cushion. Cowhide Covers $13.35. Roan skin $12.35. Height 42 inches. Seat 21x22 inches. Legs 2½ inches square. Shipping weight 100 pounds.

H9 Rocker

Come-Packt Price $11.95. Dealer's price $21.00. Imperial Leather Auto-Spring Cushion. Cowhide Cover $16.90. Roan skin $16.40. Height 42 inches. Seat 21x22 inches. Legs 2½ inches square. Shipping weight 100 pounds.

Come-Packt Morris Chairs

Talk about solid comfort! You'll find it, in generous measure, in the cushioned luxury of a COME-PACKT Morris Chair!

No Living Room, Library or Den is complete without one or more of these hospitable, roomy Morris Chairs, whose very appearance is an invitation.

The designs of these chairs gives the impression of massiveness, yet they are not too heavy for convenient handling. For smoking, reading or "just resting," there is nothing more thoroughly comfortable than a COME-PACKT Morris Chair.

H15 Reclining Chair

Come-Packt Price $16.75. Imperial Leather Auto-Spring Cushions. Dealer's price $33.00. Cowhide Covers $23.30. Roan skin $22.85. Height 43 inches. Width 33¾ inches. Depth 32 inches. Shipping weight 140 pounds.

H40 Morris Chair

Come-Packt Price $12.75. Dealer's price $20.50. (Imperial leather Auto-Spring Cushion.) Cowhide Covers $20.25. Roan skin $17.75. Seat 21x22½ inches. Back 27x19 inches. Legs 1⅝ inches square. Adjustable back. Shipping weight 100 pounds. A splendid companion piece for our Modern Mission designs

H1 Morris Chair

Come-Packt Price $14.15. Imperial Leather Auto-Spring Cushions. Dealer's price $23.50. Cowhide Covers $22.95. Roan skin $19.90. Seat 23x24 inches. Back 22x28 inches. Legs 2½ inches square. Adjustable back. Shipping weight 110 pounds.

Who Makes It? Who Stands Back of Its Quality?

It is not enough for us or for anyone to CLAIM quality,—we must demonstrate it, prove it, live up to it. A Manufacturer who Trade-Marks and Advertises his products cannot evade this responsibility. The time to think this over is BEFORE you buy. We as Manufacturers are DIRECTLY responsible to you as buyer. We cannot evade our responsibility, if we would.

Auto-Spring Cushions

The first forty-five pages of this catalog are devoted to our SECTIONAL furniture. All designs requiring cushions are provided with our new type of AUTO-SPRING CUSHION. (See descriptive matter on page 7.)

Refer to index on page 6 for quick reference to other catalog numbers or classes of furniture. Write for delivered prices on the pieces you contemplate buying,—see just how much money can be saved by buying direct from our Factories.

H16 Morris Chair

Come-Packt Price $13.75. (Imperial Leather Auto-Spring Cushions). Dealer's price $38.00. Cowhide Covers $22.50. Roan skin $19.50. Seat 24x22 inches. Legs 2½ inches square. Back cushion 21½x31½ inches. Adjustable back. Shipping weight 115 pounds.

H58 Morris Chair

Come-Packt Price $10.25. Dealer's price $17.50. Imperial Leather Auto-Spring Cushions. Cowhide Covers $18.65. Roan skin $17.95. Seat 21x21½ inches. Back 21x28 inches. Legs 1⅝ inches square. Adjustable back. Shipping weight 100 pounds.

H2 Morris Chair

Come-Packt Price $13.50. Imperial Leather Auto-Spring Cushions. Dealer's price $21.00. Cowhide Covers $22.25. Roan skin $19.25. Seat 23x24 inches. Back 22x28 inches. Legs 2½ inches square. Adjustable back. Shipping weight 110 pounds.

Better Furniture for Your Home

Good furniture is a refining, uplifting influence, a factor in **character building.** The same degree of care should be exercised in its selection as in the choosing of books.

The best traditions of the furniture craftsman are upheld in C O M E - P A C K T Furniture.

It is simple, restful, free from freakish outlines or garish ornamentation.

C O M E - P A C K T is so reasonably priced that everyone can afford it. Whether you purchase enough of it to completely furnish your home *now,* or add a piece at a time as circumstances permit is a mere matter of detail.

Many of our customers make a practice of adding one or more pieces of C O M E - P A C K T Furniture on Birthday and Wedding anniversaries, at Christmas, etc. Try this plan.

H29 Rocker

Come-Packt Price $11.25. Dealer's price $21.50. Imperial Leather Auto-Spring cushions. Cowhide Covers $14.15. Roan skin $13.15. Height 35 inches. Seat 21x21½ inches. Shipping weight 105 pounds.

H30 Chair

Come-Packt Price $10.75. Dealer's price $21.00. Imperial Leather Auto-Spring cushions. Cowhide Covers $13.65. Roan skin $12.65. Legs 2½ inches square. These chairs match the H200 suit, H300 table and bed davenport H213. Shipping weight 100 pounds.

H74 Chair

Come-Packt Price $9.95. (Cane panel and seat only). Dealer's price $14.50. Height 32½ inches. Seat 20x18½ inches. Width 23 inches. Shipping weight 70 pounds.

H201 Settee

Come-Packt Price $17.95. Imperial Leather Auto-Spring Cushions. Dealer's price $32.00. Cowhide Covers $26.25. Roan Skin $23.55. Back pads for Nos. 200 or 201 (Imperial leather), $2.75 each. Cowhide $5.50 each. Roan skin $4.75 each. Height 31 inches. Width 54 inches. Depth 30 inches. Cushions 50x27 inches x 4½ inches. Posts 2½ inches. Shipping weight 160 pounds.

H75 Rocker

Come-Packt Price $10.55. (Cane panel and seat only). Dealer's price $15.00. Height 32½ inches Seat 20x18½ inches. Width 23 inches. Shipping weight 70 pounds.

H202 Davenport

Come-Packt Price $23.85. Imperial Leather Auto-Spring Seat Cushions only. Dealer's price $48.00. Cowhide Covers $36.60. Roan skin $32.25. Back pads (Imperial leather), $2.75 each. Cowhide $5.59 each. Roan skin $4.75 each. Height 31 inches. Length 79 inches. Depth 30 inches. Cushions 75x27 inches. Posts 2½ inches. Shipping weight 225 pounds.

H200 Corner Chair

Come-Packt Price $12.45. (Imperial Leather Auto-Spring Seat Cushion only. Dealer's price $19.00. Cowhide Cover $16.75. Roan skin $15.25. Height 31 inches. Width 30 inches. Depth 30 inches. Seat 25x27 inches. Legs 2½ inches square. Shipping weight 100 pounds Back Pad Imperial Leather $2.75 extra. Cowhide $5.50. Roan skin $4.75.

Quarter Sawn White Oak

H220 Bungalow Chair

Come-Packt Price $15.70. (Imperial Leather Auto-Spring Cushions). Retail value $25.50. Cowhide Covers $18.70. Roan skin $17.45. Height 33 inches. Width 29 inches. Seat 22x21½ inches. Shipping weight 90 pounds.

H221 Bungalow Rocker

Come-Packt Price $16.25. (Imperial Leather Auto-Spring Cushions). Retail value $25.00. Cowhide Covers $19.25. Roan skin $17.95. Height 33 inches. Width 29 inches. Seat 22x21½ inches. Shipping weight 90 pounds.

H222 Bungalow Settee

Come-Packt Price $22.75. (Imperial Leather Auto-Spring Cushions). Retail value $38.00. Cowhide Covers $29.35. Roan Skin $27.70. Height 33 inches. Width 52 inches. Shipping weight 140 pounds.

H217 Craftsman Chair

H218 Craftsman Rocker

H219 Craftsman Settee

A great many have thought that a design to be in the true Mission style must necessarily be heavy and bulky. The primitive designs brought back from the old California Missions were large and massive in construction, but this was due to a lack of proper tools for making better or more artistic pieces of furniture. Modern designers have modified the parts of the original pieces that were out of proportion, and too clumsy to be useful or ornamental in a modern home.

The three piece suit shown above has all the characteristics of the early Mission pieces, but with right proportions,—the pieces are comfortable and of a size that will not be out of place wherever they may be used. They are 33 inches high and the settee is 52 inches wide. Shipping weight Settee 150 pounds. Chair 95 pounds. These pieces are invariably shipped in sections unless ordered assembled. A handsome quarter sawn white oak suit like this would easily sell for $75.00.

COME-PACKT PRICE		Imperial Leather	Cowhide	Roan Skin
H217	Chair	$11.55	$14.60	$13.40
H218	Rocker	12.15	15.15	13.90
H219	Settee	17.60	24.25	22.50

H204 Modern Mission Chair

Come-Packt Price $9.45. Imperial Leather Auto-Spring Cushions. Dealer's price $20.00. Cowhide Cushions, $12.45. Roan skin $11.50. Height 33 inches. Width 25 inches. Depth 25½ inches. Seat 21x21½ inches. Legs 1⅝ inches square. Shipping weight 100 pounds.

H205 Modern Mission Rocker

Come-Packt Price $9.95. Imperial leather Auto-Spring Cushions. Dealer's price $21.00. Cowhide Covers $12.95. Roan skin $11.95. Height 32 inches. Width 25 inches. Depth 25½ inches. Seat 21x21½ inches. Legs 1⅝ inches square. Shipping weight 105 pounds.

H206 Modern Mission Settee

Come-Packt Price $15.95. (Imperial leather Auto-Spring Cushions. Dealer's price $35.00. Cowhide Covers $22.65. Roan skin $20.50. Height 33 inches. Length 52 inches. Depth 25½ inches. Legs 1⅝ inches square. Shipping weight 160 pounds.

Quarter Sawn White Oak

A COME-PACKT Davenport is one of the most useful and altogether desirable pieces of furniture you can buy. It provides the seating capacity of three or four chairs, and serves the double purpose of couch and bed. It is much more practical than a built-in window seat. Our Davenports are exceptionally artistic in design, very strong and serviceable, and the resilient Spring Cushions add the finishing touch of perfection.

A COME-PACKT Davenport will prove a most appropriate and convenient part of the appointments of your Living Room, Hall, Library or Den. Note the low prices.

NOTE—Auto Spring Cushions for Settees and Davenports are made in one piece only.

H602 Den Couch

H203 Davenport

H602 Den Couch
Come-Packt Price $20.65. Imperial Leather Auto-Spring Cushion. Dealer's price $38.00. Cowhide Covers $33.55. Roan skin $28.95 extra. Length 80 inches. Width 30 inches. Shipping weight 225 pounds.

H203 Davenport
Come-Packt Price $19.85. Imperial Leather Auto-Spring Cushion. Dealer's price $35.00. Cowhide Covers $29.75. Roan skin $26.35. Height 32 inches. Length 69 inches. Depth 25½ inches. Legs 1⅝ inches square. Shipping weight 190 pounds.

H223 Corner Chair

Come-Packt Price $9.65. Imperial Leather Auto-Spring Cushions. Dealer's price $15.50. Cowhide Covers $12.95. Roan skin $11.85. Height 32 inches. Seat 21x23½ inches. Legs 1⅝ inches square. Shipping weight 95 pounds.

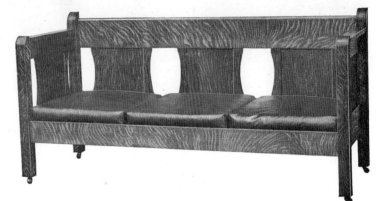

H224 Davenport

Come-Packt Price $27.45. (Imperial Leather Auto-Spring Cushions). Retail value $55.00. Cowhide Covers $39.60. Roan skin $34.45. Height 38 inches. Width 78 inches. Seat 73½x27 ins. Depth 29 inches. Posts 2½ inches. Shipping weight 250 pounds.

No. 207 Davenport

H207 Davenport

Come-Packt Price $23.85. Imperial Leather Auto-Spring Seat Cushion only. Dealer's price $47.00. Cowhide Covers $36.60. Roan skin $32.25 extra. Back pads. (Imperial leather), $2.75 each. Cowhide $5.50 each. Roan skin $4.75 each. Height 38 inches. Width 80 inches. Depth 30 inches. Posts 2½ inches. Shipping weight 250 pounds.

The Manufacturer or Dealer that offers you "Solid Oak" and does not say whether it is Red, White, Plain or Quarter Sawn, is attempting to deceive you—he hopes that you do not know the difference.

Quarter Sawn White Oak

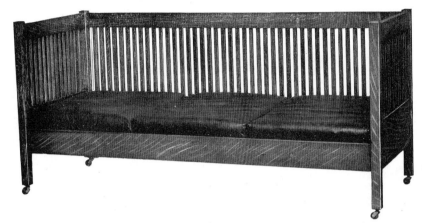

H215 Davenport

H215 Davenport

Come-Packt Price $22.25. Dealer's price $39.00. (Imperial Leather Auto-Spring Cushion). Cowhide Covers $32.15. Roan skin $28.75. Height 32 inches. Length 69 inches. Depth 25½ inches. Legs 1⅝ inches square. Shipping weight 170 pounds. Spring cushions made in one piece only for all davenports.

H216 Corner Chair

Come-Packt Price $10.90. Dealer's price $16.50. (Imperial Leather Auto-Spring Cushion). Cowhide Cover $14.25. Roan skin $13.15. Height 32 inches. Seat 21x23½ inches. Legs 1⅝ inches square. Shipping weight 95 pounds.

H211 Couch

Come-Packt Price $19.50. (Imperial Leather Auto-Spring Cushion). Cowhide Covers $32.25. Roan skin $27.90. Dealer's price $45.00. Height 26 inches. Length 80 inches. Depth 30 inches. Legs 2½ inches square. Couches H211 and H212 are identical except in length. Shipping weight 225 pounds.

H212 Couch

Come-Packt Price $15.25. (Imperial Leather Auto-Spring Cushion). Cowhide Covers $23.75. Roan skin $20.85. Dealer's price $35.00. Height 26 inches. Length 57 inches. Depth 30 inches. Shipping weight 170 pounds. Cushions in one piece only.

H210 Davenport

Come-Packt Price $25.50. (Imperial Leather Auto-Spring Seat Cushion only). Dealer's price $70.00. Cowhide Covers, $38.25. Roan skin $33.90. Back Pads, (3) Imperial leather, $8.25 extra. Cowhide, $16.50. Roan skin, $14.25. Height 38 inches. Width 80 inches. Depth 30 inches. Seat cushions one piece only. Shipping weight 250 pounds

H208 Corner Chair

Come-Packt Price $11.75. (Imperial Leather Auto-Spring Seat Cushion only). Dealer's price $28.50. Cowhide $15.95. Roan skin $13.55. Back Pad Imperial Leather, $2.75 extra. Cowhide $5.50. Roan skin $4.75. Height 38 inches. Width 31 inches. Depth 30 inches. Seat cushion 26½x24½ inches.

Quarter Sawn White Oak

Gate End Davenport Beds

The gate-end **Davenport Bed** must be seen to appreciate all of the real beauty and merit of this exceptionally fine piece of furniture. Its appearance as a Davenport gives no hint of its possibilities as a bed, and yet it is full fifty inches wide when opened out and is in reality as perfect a bed in appearance and as comfortable as any bed could be. A dust-proof box provides a place for the bedding by day, and the upholstered spring cushion insures the restful comfort that a bed should possess. There are no objectionable features and nothing to get out of order. It is a perfect bed and a perfect Davenport at the price of one piece. Each cushion is in reality a combination of a half size high grade bed spring with a mattress top. Sixty-five oil tempered high carbon steel hour glass springs in each cushion insuring the maximum of elasticity and comfort.

Invest your money—don't merely spend it. Buy furniture from the viewpoint of service.

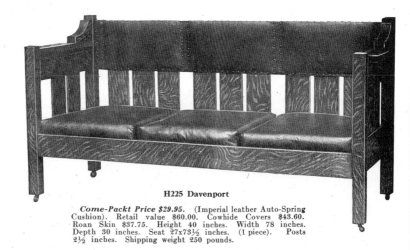

H225 Davenport

Come-Packt Price $29.95. (Imperial leather Auto-Spring Cushion). Retail value $60.00. Cowhide Covers $43.60. Roan Skin $37.75. Height 40 inches. Width 78 inches. Depth 30 inches. Seat 27x73½ inches. (1 piece). Posts 2½ inches. Shipping weight 250 pounds.

H241 Open as a Bed

Come-Packt Price $47.50. Dealer's price $70.00. (Figured denim cloth. Samples on request). Imperial leather covers $49.50. Cowhide Covers $64.50. Roan skin can be furnished only by making two or more welt seams on each cushion, price $59.25. Dimensions same as for H231 below. Shipping weight 400 pounds.

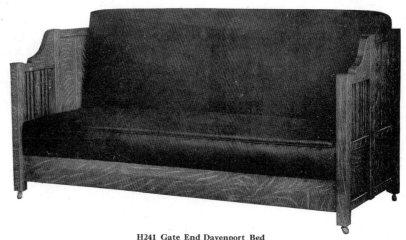

H241 Gate End Davenport Bed

When no stain or cushion materials are specified in an order we will furnish dark weathered stain and brown natural grain Imperial Leather.

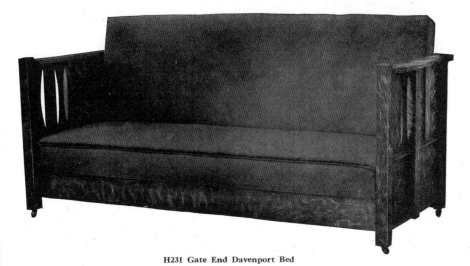

H231

Come-Packt Price $46.75. In figured denim cloth. Samples sent on request. Imperial leather Covers $48.95. Cowhide Covers $63.75. Roan skin $58.50. Each cushion 75 inches long, 25 inches wide. Height of ends 34 inches. Length over all 82¼ inches. As a Davenport the front post stands 38½ inches from wall. Height of back cushion (as davenport) 39 inches.

H231 Gate End Davenport Bed

The Great Thorobed

Designers and mechanics have been striving for years to perfect a bed davenport that would excell all other devices on the market, and at the same time fill the requirements for this particular article of furniture. In the Thorobed, we have a perfect bed (not a makeshift) and a perfect davenport, a handsome and durable piece of furniture for either or both purposes. The mechanism is so simple and perfect in operation that you must see the davenport to believe that so excellent an article could be made. There is nothing to get out of order, or wear out in constant service. You will appreciate the beauty, utility and the life-time of service that the Thorobed will give you. The helical springs and connecting flexible steel web give the maximum of comfort and service; a better spring could not be devised for this type of a bed. Your choice of our regular Mission finishes.

H4421

No. H4421 Come-Packt Price, (Imperial leather) Quartered Oak only $48.75. Cowhide, $65.50. This thorobed is not upholstered in roan skin, the hides are too small to make up well on these large cushions.

The spindle ends make a pleasing mission design in any of our finishes and the easy rolling arm rests do not appear incongruous in a room furnished entirely in the straight line pure mission designs. It is impossible to make the arm rests in solid quartered oak—they are veneered over solid oak as is the front and back rail. Any desired combination of cushions can be made for any of these Thorobeds, either smooth as shown in the illustration, or tufted seat and back or tufted seat only as shown in the Nos. 4403 or 4405 on the following page.

Be sure to specify the kind wanted or the plain cushions will be shipped on your order. Cotton Felt Mattress 6 x 4 feet, $3.75 extra. Width, 58 inches. Height, 37 inches. Shipping weight, 340 pounds.

No. H4401 Thorobed (same design as No. 4421 except 80 inches wide). Come-Packt price, (Imperial leather,) $49.50. Cowhide, $69.75. Shipping weight, 380 pounds. Cotton Felt Mattress 6 x 4 feet, $3 75 extra.

No. H4422 Come-Packt Price, (Imperial leather) Quartered Oak only $44.90. Cowhide Covers, $57.50. This design not made up in roan skins. This splendid piece and the No. 4402 on the following page are designed especially to harmonize with our regular Come-Packt pieces, the true Mission effect has been faithfully carried out in every detail. The completed settee or davenport cannot fail to please you with their sturdy dignified proportions and pleasing outlines. No wardrobe is provided with this design and the pillows and extra bedding must be stored elsewhere. The frame is solid quarter sawn white oak and the mechanism is the same as for all settee size Thorobeds. They open out as illustrated below in the small cuts.

The smooth cushions only should be used with these straight lined designs. Width, 58 inches. Height, 37 inches. Shipping weight, 340 pounds. Cotton Felt Mattress 4 x 6 feet, $3.75 extra.

H4422

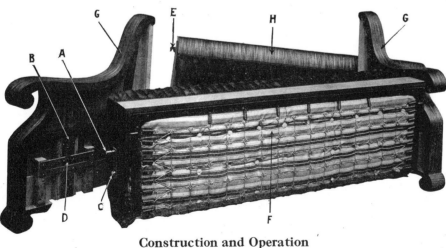

Construction and Operation

Illustration "J"

Illustration "K"

Illustration "L"

All Davenport beds are invariably shipped in sections. It is the work of only a few minutes to assemble them. Follow carefully the instructions for assembling and then, if at any time it should be necessary to take them apart, you will find that this operation is equally simple.

Turn the bed section "F" with front rail up as shown above. Take end sections "G" in the position as shown and insert the metal dowell "A" in slot "B" and at the same time insert the lug "C" at slot "D." Follow same instructions at the opposite end of davenport and then turn the section "F" into its natural position with cushion on top as it will be when used as a davenport. The back section "H" will next be placed in position by slipping the metal plates "E" into position over blue head screws that you will find already in place. (These davenports have all been assembled before shipping out so that there is no possibility of getting them together in any way except the right way.) Secure the back firmly to the end sections by putting a screw through the small hole provided for it in the metal plate "E". The back section contains a wardrobe for pillows, (except in the Mission designs Nos. 4402 and 4422.

TO MAKE UP AS A BED—Lift up on front rail and the seat will revolve into position shown in illustration "J". Turn the round metal latch which holds spring in place, and unfolding the hinged portion of spring, let down the metal legs and bed will appear as shown in illustration "K". When made up as a bed the Settee size will appear as in illustration "L", but the full length size will unfold but once and the bed will extend the long way of the davenport.

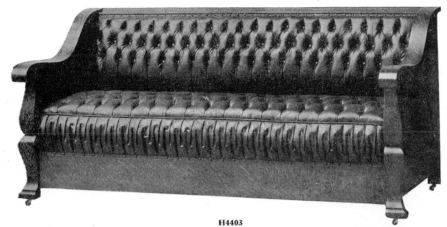

H4403

No. H4403 Come-Packt Price (Imperial leather), Quartered Oak or Mahoganized Birch, $54.50. Cowhide Covers, $69.75. Roan skins cannot be used satisfactorily on these large pieces. This is a handsome design either in Oak or Mahoganized Birch,—the lines are pleasing and graceful and the ruffled front of the seat cushion together with the diamond tufting will be particularly desirable in a room with other pieces similarly upholstered. The arm, front and back rails are laminated solid oak or in the Birch are solid without veneering.

When ordering specify whether oak or birch is wanted. The cushions as shown will be made up unless you especially request smooth, or part smooth cushions. Oak will invariably be sent unless otherwise ordered. Width, 80 inches. Height, 37 inches. Shipping weight, 380 pounds. Cottonfelt mattress, $3.75 extra.

No. H4423 Come-Packt Price $51.50. (Imperial leather.) Cowhide Covers, $68.50. Same design as above except in 58-inch length. Shipping weight, 380 pounds. 4 x 6 Cotton Felt Mattress, $3.75 extra.

No. H4404 Thorobed Come-Packt Price (Imperial Leather) Plain Oak or Mahoganized Birch $38.25. Cowhide covers, $56.75. These thorobeds are so entirely different from the ordinary davenport bed, that it is hard to describe all of their excellent qualities, or to show the splendid values in an illustration. This particular design is made in the plain sawn oak (except the front rail which is quartered veneer over the plain oak) and is intended for those who want the convenience of these davenports at a lower price than is possible with the quarter sawn oak. The claw feet add a touch of ornamentation that is in pleasing contrast to the severe lines of the Mission style. The cushions may be made up in the tufted seat and back or a tufted seat and plain back, be sure to specify if you wish cushions other than those shown in the illustration. Width, 80 inches, Height, 37 inches. Shipping Weight, 380 pounds. Cottonfelt Mattress $3.75 extra.

No. H4424 Thorobed Come-Packt Price (Imperial leather) $36.75. Cowhide, $55.50. Same design as No. H4004, except in settee width (58 inches). Shipping Weight, 240 pounds. Mattress 6 x 4 feet, $3.75 extra.

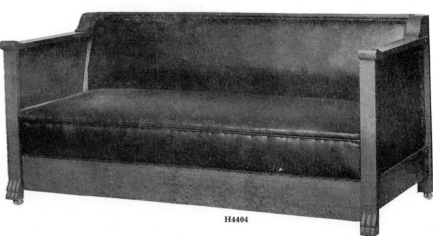

H4404

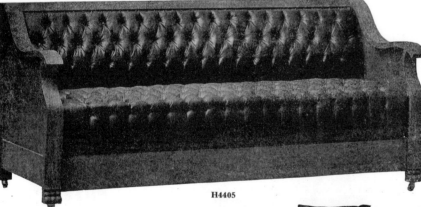

H4405

No. H4405 Thorobed Come-Packt Price (Imperial leather), Quartered Oak or Mahoganized Birch, $48.75. Cowhide Covers, $65.75. The splendid quality of design and workmanship will be appreciated by everyone who admires a well balanced piece of furniture. Your choice of Quarter Sawn laminated Oak or Mahoganized Birch at a price that ought to be attractive. It is our endeavor at all times to not only give good values, but to give better values than can be obtained by buying through the old channels. Compare values as well as prices because Price is not always a measure of Value as it should be. The claw feet and gracefully curved arms and posts, the diamond tufted cushions, all combine to produce an unusually attractive design. While the illustration shows the tufted cushions, only, you have a choice of smooth or half smooth cushions. Do not neglect to specify the kind if you prefer the tufted style. The quartered oak will be shipped unless you specify Mahoganized Birch. Cotton felt mattress 6 x 4 feet, $3.75 extra. Width, 80 inches. Height, 37 inches. Shipping weight, 380 pounds.

No. H4425 Thorobed Come-Packt Price Quartered Oak or Mahoganized Birch, (Imperial leather) $47.75. Cowhide Covers, $64.75. This design is the same as H4405 except that it is the settee width (58 inches). Shipping weight, 340 pounds. Cotton felt Mattress, $3.75 extra.

No. H4402 Thorobed Come-Packt Price (Imperial leather) $47.50. Cowhide Covers, $59.75. Quartered Oak only. (Pillows not included.) This handsome Mission piece is the same design as the No. H4422 on the preceding page, and is shown here to illustrate the difference between the settee and davenport sizes. Both styles have the same size spring and mattress but, of course, open up differently. It is a matter of choice whether the large or small size is to be used, the settee is, of course, intended for smaller rooms or where the wall space will not permit the 80-inch length. There is comparatively little difference in cost between the different lengths as the mechanism of the settee costs more than for the davenport and this difference compensates for the added cost of materials used in the davenport. Both styles are equally comfortable and easy to operate. Length, 80 inches. Height, 37 inches. Shipping weight, 380 pounds. Cottonfelt Mattress $3.75 extra.

H4402

Quartered White Oak

H700 Hall Mirror
Come-Packt Price $6.75. Dealer's price $12.50. Width 40½ inches. Height 21 inches. French bevel plate mirror 14x24 inches. Two double and three single hooks included. Shipping weight 60 pounds.

A Man is judged as much by the furnishings in his home as well as by the clothes he wears or the friends he cultivates—it does not cost as much to have Come-Packt furniture in your home as the "near" furniture, and its quality and appearance calls for no apology.

H710 Costumer
Come-Packt Price $7.50. Dealer's price $15.00. Height 67 inches. Four large Antique Copper Hooks included. Shipping weight 75 pounds.

H720 Hall Settee
Come-Packt Price $12.15. Dealer's price $19.50. Height 39 inches. Length 42½ inches. Depth 22 inches. Shipping weight 90 pounds.

H705 Costumer
Come-Packt Price $4.75. Dealer's price $8.50. Height 67 inches. Four Antique Copper Hooks included. Shipping weight 60 pounds.

H706 Costumer
Come-Packt Price $6.75. Dealer's price $9.75. Height 66 inches. Six Antique Copper Hooks included. Shipping weight 65 pounds.

H708 Hall Mirror
Come-Packt Price $6.95. (Including French bevel plate mirror). Dealer's price $16.00. Height 24 inches. Width 39½ inches. Mirror 24x14 inches. Two large and 3 single Copper Hooks included. Shipping weight 60 pounds.

Solid quarter sawn white oak is one basis for comparison of quality.

H709 Umbrella Stand
Come-Packt Price $5.75. Dealer's price $12.00. Height 31 inches. Width 18 inches. Depth 13 inches. Shipping weight 55 pounds.

H704 Umbrella Stand
Come-Packt Price $3.45. Dealer's price $6.75. Height 31½ inches. 13¾ inches square. Shipping weight 45 pounds.

H707 Settee
Come-Packt Price $12.75. (Dealer's price $22.00. Height 37 inches. Width 42½ inches. Depth 20 inches. Shipping weight 90 pounds.

H721 Hall Chest
Come-Packt Price $11.75. Dealer's price $17.00. Height 21 inches. Length 40 inches. Depth 21 inches. Red cedar lining $3.00 extra. Shipping weight 130 pounds. Inside dimensions 36x16x18 deep.

H703 Hall Chair
Come-Packt Price $5.65. Dealer's price $9.50. Height 44 inches. Seat 17½x17 inches. Shipping weight 50 pounds.

Quarter Sawn White Oak

We own and operate our own factories and the only steps between you and the rough lumber are our machine and packing rooms—there can never be any greater economy than this.

H438 Foot Stool

Come-Packt Price $3.45. Dealer's price $6.75. (Imperial leather cushion). Cowhide Top $4.45. Roan skin $4.20 extra. Shipping weight 30 pounds.

H409 Window Seat

Come-Packt Price $6.95. Dealer's price $12.25. Height 28 inches. Width 33½ inches. Depth 19½ inches. Storage room under cover. Shipping weight 65 pounds.

H711 Window Seat

Come-Packt Price $6.90. Dealer's price $12.50. (Imperial leather pad cushions). Cowhide covers $9.20. Roan skin $8.40. Extreme height 27½ inches. Width 28 inches. Depth 19 inches. Shipping weight 50 pounds.

H503, 504 and 506 Porch Swings

These three swings are identical except in length. The price in each case includes Denim Cushions. With every swing we send 36 feet of heavy galvanized iron chain, hooks and everything ready to put up. These swings are made of plain sawn white oak.

No. H503, Length, 49 inches. Shipping weight 130 pounds. **Come-Packt Price $6.75.** No. H 504, Length 61 inches. Shipping weight 150 pounds. **Come-Packt Price $8.75.** No. H506, Length 73 inches. Shipping weight 160 pounds. **Come-Packt Price $10.25.**

H43 Reception Chair

Come-Packt Price $3.95. Imperial leather. Dealer's price $7.25. Cowhide or Roan skin Covers 50 cents extra each. Shipping weight 35 pounds.

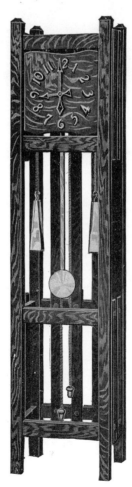

H2020 Hall Clock

Come-Packt Price $24.95. Dealer's price $35.00. Height 78 inches. Width 18½ inches. Dial 12 inches. Movement 8-day, half-hour strike, cathedral gong. Shipping weight 95 pounds.

H432 Paper Basket or Palm Stand

Come-Packt Price $3.80. Dealer's price $6.50. Height 19 inches. Top 15x15 inches. Bottom 13x13 inches.

This piece may be packed with other furniture, and the freight will be next to nothing on it. Shipping weight 35 pounds.

H418

Come-Packt Price $3.75. Dealer's price $7.00. Imperial leather cushion. Cowhide, $4.60. Roan skin $4.30. Height 15 inches Top 20x15 inches. Shipping weight 40 pounds.

H417 Foot Stool

Come-Packt Price $3.10. Dealer's price $6.50. Imperial leather top. Cowhide top, $4.85. Roan skin, $4.35. Height 15 inches. Top 23x14 inches. Shipping weight 40 pounds.

H2025 Mantel Clock

Come-Packt Price $5.00. Dealer's price $9.50. Height 14½ inches. Width 11¾ inches. Dial 6 inches. Movement 8-day. Cathedral gong. Shipping weight 25 pounds.

Quarter Sawn White Oak

H435 Cellarette

Come-Packt Price $6.25. Dea.er s price $12.00. Height 28 inches. 1 shelf arranged inside. Drawer 7x8x3 inches deep. Shipping weight 60 pounds.

H41 Reception Chair

Come-Packt Price $4.75. Imperial leather, Dealer's price $7.75. Cowhide or Roan skin Covers 50 cents extra each. Height 37 inches. Legs 1⅜ inches. Seat 15x16 inches. Shipping weight 35 pounds.

H42 Nursery Rocker

Come-Packt Price $4.90. Dealer's price $8.00. (Choice of Imperial leather or cane seat). Cowhide or Roan skin Covers 50 cents extra. Shipping weight 40 pounds.

H408 Cellarette

Come-Packt Price $4.75. Dealer's price $8.00. Height 28½ inches. Width 19 inches. Depth 11½ inches. Shipping weight 80 p. unds.

H666 Chifforobe

Come-Packt Price $28.50. Price includes umbrella rack, scarf holder and extension rod for clothes hooks. The Chifforobe can be furnished without interior drawer section for $24 25. Dealer's price $45.00. Height 5 feet 6 inches. Width 40 inches. Depth 21 inches. Lock on door.

The Chifforobe is as "handy as a pocket in a coat," and not only a convenience but almost a necessity in a bedroom where closet space is limited. It does away with a chiffonier and at the same time provides ample room for hanging clothes, dresses and other apparel and boots and shoes. Shipping weight 270 pounds.

H440 Music Cabinet

Come-Packt Price $12.30. Dealer's price $18.00. Three distinct interior arrangements have been made to accommodate disc phonograph records, cylinder records, piano player records or sheet music. Specify kind desired when ordering. Height 37 inches. Top 22x16 inches. Shipping weight 125 pounds.

We will be glad to have you write to us of your requirements in furniture, and we can possibly be of assistance in making recommendations of suitable designs and finishes for your rooms.

GREATLY PLEASED
The furniture shipped me reached here in fine condition and the least I can say is I am GREATLY PLEASED with the goods.
Mr. M. E. KIMSEY
R. R. No. 1, Pleasant Lake, Ind.
June 8, 1912

H400 Screen

Come-Packt Price $9.25. (W thout Panels). Dealers price $22.00. Denim covered panels each, 75 cents extra. Height 72 inches. Each section 20 inches wide. Imperial leather panels each, $1.50 extra. Shipping weight 110 pounds.

H312 Library Table

Come-Packt Price $5.85. Dealer's price $9.50. Height 30 inches. Top 30 inches. Shipping weight 70 pounds.

H625 Child's Dresser

Come-Packt Price $14.25. Dealer's price $25.00. Old Brass Drawer Pulls. Shipping weight 130 pounds. This dresser is suitable for children up to 10 or 12 years of age. Later it may be used without mirror as a shirt waist box.

NOTHING TO PAY FOR BUT QUALITY

H62 Piano Seat

Come-Packt Price $12.50. (Solid Mahogany, Dull Finish or Piano Polish). Dealer's price $18.50. Height 21½ inches. Top 36x16 inches. Compartment under seat for sheet music. Shipping weight 45 pounds.

H44 Reception Chair

Come-Packt Price $4.25. Dealer's price $7.50. (Choice of imperial leather or cane seat). Cowhide or Roan skin Covers 50 cents each extra. Shipping weight 35 pounds.

H63 Piano Seat

Come-Packt Price $8.15. Quartered Oak. Dealer's price $14.50. Height 21½ inches. Top 36x16 inches. Compartment under seat for sheet music. Shipping weight 45 pounds.

H437 Tabourette

Come-Packt Price $3.90. Dealer's price $6.75. Height 27 inches. Top 15½x14½ inches. Shipping weight 35 pounds.

H474 Pedestal

Come-Packt Price $6.25. Dealer's price $10.50. Height 38 inches. Top 15x15 inches. Base 16x16 inches. Shipping weight 60 pounds.

H475 Pedestal

Come-Packt Price $7.25. Dealer's price $11.50. Height 38 inches. Top 15x15 inches. Base 16x16 inches. Shipping weight 65 pounds.

H404 Book Shelves

Come-Packt Price $5.90. Dealer's price $11.00. Height 38 inches. Width 25 inches. Depth 14½ inches. Shipping weight 65 pounds.

H416 Plant Stand

Come-Packt Price $4.75. Dealer's price $9.50. Height 35 inches. 15½x15¾ inches square Shipping weight 50 pounds.

H403 Tabourette

Come-Packt Price $3.45. Dealer's price $6.50. Height 28 inches. 15x15 inches square. Shipping weight 45 pounds.

H453 Book Case

A great many housekeepers will appreciate the convenience offered by the ample drawer room in this case. Private papers, and odds and ends that accumulate, but are too valuable to be thrown away find a ready resting place here. The design is simple but tasty. Height 58 inches. Width 42 inches. Four adjustable shelves. Glass 28x14 inches. Shipping weight 220 pounds. Dealer's price $35.00. *Come-Packt Price $24.60* (Without glass). Glass inserted $25.40.

![SECTIONAL "COME-PACKT" FURNITURE]

**Quartered
White
Oak**

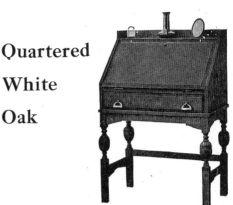

H357 Ladies' Desk

Come-Packt Price $12.70. Dealer's price $21.00. Height 43 inches. Width 30 inches. Depth 17 inches. Choice of Old Brass or Wood Drawer Pulls. Pigeon holes arranged to accommodate papers, envelopes and writing materials. Shipping weight 105 pounds.

H358 Ladies' Desk

Come-Packt Price $8.60. Dealer's price $15.00. Height 41 inches. Width 21 inches. Depth 15½ inches. One drawer 24x13x4 inches. Pigeon holes arranged to accommodate writing materials. Shipping weight 85 pounds.

H332 Ladies' Writing Desk

Come-Packt Price $10.75. Dealer's price $28.25. Height 43 inches. Width 30 inches. Depth 17 inches. Convenient pigeon holes are arranged to accommodate envelopes, writing paper, etc. Shipping weight 120 pounds.

H321 Ladies' Writing Desk

Come-Packt Price $10.50. Dealer's price $17.00. Height 45 inches. Width 29 inches. Depth 17 inches. Old Brass Trimmings. Pigeon holes are conveniently arranged inside for writing materials, etc. Shipping weight 120 pounds.

H379 Ladies' Desk

Come-Packt Price $14.25. Dealer's price $25.00. Height 42 inches. Top 8x28 inches. Drawers 27x13x4 inches. Gliding casters put on all pieces not provided with roll casters. Shipping weight 115 pounds.

H380 Ladies' Desk

Come-Packt Price $11.25. Dealer's price $18.50. Height 43 inches. Top 7½x28 inches. Legs 1⅝ inches. Drawer 23x14½x4 inches. Shipping weight 110 pounds.

Why not keep the unnecessary profits and expenses in your own pocket?

H455 Book Case

A glimpse of this beautiful Mission design through the eye of the camera does not do justice to the actual appearance of the piece as it looks when finished. The plain square knobs are in keeping with the style of this piece. Height 57 inches. Width 64 knobs. Shelves 12½ inches deep Shipping weight 290 pounds. Ordinary retail price for this class of case $60.00. *Come-Packt Price $36.35.* (Without glass), Glass inserted $38.65. (3) large glasses 16x33. Small glass 16x8 inches.

H450 Book Case

The same splendid lines as shown in our H451 case, but this is made in the single door width. Height of case 53 inches. Width 26 inches. Glass 19x39 inches. Shipping weight 135 pounds. Ordinary retail price $19.50. Come-Packt Price $12.70 (Without glass). Glass inserted $13.45.

H32 Desk Chair

Come-Packt Price $4.75. Dealer's price $9.50. Height 32½ inches Legs 1¾ inches. This chair is a companion piece for any desk. Shipping weight 50 pounds.

Page twenty-four

Quartered White Oak

BOOK CASES

The simple elegance of these Book-Cases is strictly in keeping with the canons of good taste.   They are admirably designed and built with the extreme care and attention to detail which characterizes all COME-PACKT cabinet-making.

House your literary treasures in book-cases that, in every outline, suggests culture and refinement.   Among the various COME-PACKT styles here illustrated you will find *one particular book-case* that exactly "fits in" with the general requirements of your library or living room—*and* that fits your pocketbook as well.

H456 Book Case

The mortise and tenoned lock rails with projecting ends give this design a true Mission appearance. The two drawers are as handy as a pocket in a shirt and the evident capacity of the shelves together with the pleasing lines, makes this an attractive design for any home.

Height 58 inches. Width 37 inches. Glass 36x12 inches. Dull Brass Trimmings or Wood Knobs. Shipping weight 195 pounds. $32.50 would not be an exorbitant price for this case.

Come-Packt Price $19.75 (Without glass). Glass inserted $21.15.

H1101 Sectional Book Case

All sections are interchangeable and are identical in outside length. The sections are made in three heights, 9, 11, and 13 inches. Outside length 34 inches. Inside length 32½ inches. Depth 9½ inches. Writing desk section 15¼ inches high. H1107 Top section, $2.00. H1109 9-inch Book section $3.00. H1127 Desk section, $7.75. H1111 11-inch Book section $3.25. 1119 Base section, $2.00. H1113 13-inch Book section, $3.75. All prices include plain doors. Shipping weight, 3 book sections and one desk section, top and base, 140 pounds. Shipped knocked down.

H451 Book Case

For the Bungalow home or in a small Mission living room, it would be difficult to choose a more attractive piece than this handsome little case in solid quartered oak. It is 53 inches high by 42 inches wide, and the eight shelves afford unusual book capacity. There is an entire absence of ornamentation that gives a pleasing effect in a room furnished to harmonize in design and finish. Glass 39x19 inches. Shipping weight 180 pounds. Usual retail price $29.75. **Come-Packt Price** $17.95 (Without glass).   Glass inserted $18.85.

H454 Book Case

This is a smaller edition of the H455 and is made with the same painstaking care and finished in the best possible manner. We spare no effort to make each piece the best of its kind and our rapidly growing business shows the appreciation that our efforts have met with. Height 57 inches. Width 43 inches. Adjustable shelves. Large glass in doors 16x33 inches. Small glass 16x8 inches. Shipping weight 210 pounds. Dealer's price $37.50.   **Come-Packt Price $24.85** (Without glass).   Glass inserted $26.15.

H419 Book Case

Come-Packt Price $14.85 (Without glass).   Dealer's price $21.00. Glass inserted $16.50.   Height 54 inches.   Width 32 inches.   Depth 12 inches.   Glass (2) 12x36 inches.   Shipping weight 140 pounds.

H452 Book Case

A dignified and splendidly made "home for your books," and a large compartment for the small articles or papers. The adjustable shelves provide ample room for both large and small books. Height 56 inches. Width 40 inches. Depth 13 inches. Small glass 14x22 inches. Large 14x42 inches. Compartments 18 inches high. Shipping weight 175 pounds. Dealer's price $37.00.   **Come-Packt Price $24.45** (Without glass). Glass inserted $25.35.

H356 Writing Table

Come-Packt Price $16.45. Dealer's price $25.00. Height 30 inches. Top 44x28 inches. Legs 2¼ inches square. One drawer 22x16x3 inches deep. Old Brass Drawer Pulls. Shipping weight 135 pounds.

THE LIFE OF FURNITURE

It's the quality, not the type or design, that determines the life of furniture. We safeguard the buyer by a guarantee that insures quality and satisfaction. The beautiful and distinctive designs, the correct proportions and pleasing outlines of COME-PACKT Furniture are just so much *extra value* which add nothing to the price.

H359 Sanitary Desk

Come-Packt Price $16.65. Dealer's price $25.00. Height 30 inches. Top 48x30 inches. Six drawers which may be arranged so that the sets of three drawers will open on the opposite sides of desk. The sides of the drawers form the sides of the desk. This piece is made in plain sawn white oak only, with quartered oak top. Shipping weight 200 pounds.

H366 Library Table

Come-Packt Price $11.85. Dealer's price $18.00. Height 30 inches. Top 36x22 inches. Legs 1¾ inches square. Four book shelves 18 inches long, 8½ inches deep, 9½ inches high. Choice of Old Brass or Wood Drawer Knobs. Shipping weight 115 pounds.

H375 Sanitary Desk Table

Come-Packt Price $22.95. Dealer's price $40.00. Top Drawers only fitted with locks, fifty cents each, net extra. Height 30 inches. Top 36x52 inches. Choice of Old Brass or Wood Drawer Knobs. Shipping weight 245 pounds. All drawers 9 inches wide, 23 inches long, 6 inches deep

H447 Phone Stand and Chair

Come-Packt Price $5.75. Dealer's price $9.50. Chair seat 18 inches from floor. Price includes both pieces. Shipping weight 55 pounds.

H60 Office Chair

Come-Packt Price $9.95. Imperial leather cushion. Dealer's price $15.00. Cowhide Covers $12.70. Roan skin $12.30. Height 36 inches. Seat 17¾x18 inches. Adjustable tension on spring Shipping weight 105 pounds.

H374 Office Desk

Come-Packt Price $34.25. Dealer's price $47.50. Height 30 inches. Top 52x36 inches. Slides pull out over each top side drawer. Side drawer 9½ inches wide, 24 inches deep. Middle drawer 20x3½x24 inches. Drawers fitted with locks. Made in 3 sections. Shipping weight 275 pounds.

H61 Office Chair

Come-Packt Price $7.95. Imperial leather cushions. Cowhide Covers $9.65. Roan skin, $9.15. The two office chairs have swivel bases and are adjustable as to height. Adjustable tension on spring.

Quarter Sawn White Oak

Our manufacturing methods and selling plan place quality before you at prices which are physically, mechanically and humanly impossible under any other conditions.

H300 Library Table

Come-Packt Price $11.75. Dealer's price $25.00. Height 30 inches. Top 44x28 inches. Legs 2½ inches square. Two drawers. Choice of Old Brass or Wood Drawer Knobs. Shipping weight 150 pounds.

H351 Library Table

Come-Packt Price $12.70. Dealer's price $18.25. Height 30 inches. Top 36x26 inches. Legs 1⅝ inches square. Two drawers 5⅞x5⅞x16 inches long Choice of Old Brass or Wood Drawer Knobs. Shipping weight 120 pounds.

H376 Library Table

Come-Packt Price $16.65. Dealer's price $16.65. Height 30 inches. Top 28x44 inches. Drawer 21x16x4 inches. Back Shelves 21x8½x7 (upper), Lower Shelf 9 inches high. Old Brass Drawer Pulls. Shipping weight 150 pounds.

H377 Library Table

Come-Packt Price $16.95. Dealer's price $16.95. Height 30 inches. Top 28x44 inches. Drawers 16x15x4½ inches. Old Brass Drawer Pulls. Shipping weight 150 pounds.

H378 Library Table

Come-Packt Price $16.75. Dealer's price $16.75. Height 30 inches. Top 30x48 inches. Drawer 28½x18x4½ inches. Old Brass Drawer Pulls. Shipping weight 165 pounds.

H350 Library Table

Come-Packt Price $23.10. Dealer's price $38.00. Height 30 inches. Top 60x30. Legs 2½ inches square. Old Brass Drawer Pulls. Three drawers each 14x15½x4½ inches deep. Shipping weight 185 pounds. This table may be taken apart or assembled at any time desired.

Quartered White Oak

A point worth remembering when buying furniture is to assure yourself not only of materials used in construction but to know that it is made by a responsible concern, one whose business policy will not permit of "sharp practice," either in manufacturing or selling.

H305 Library Table

Come-Packt Price $12.35. Dealer's price $22.00. Height 30 inches. Top 48x30 inches. Legs 2½ inches square. Shipping weight 130 pounds.

H349 Bed Room Table

Come-Packt Price $7.25. Dealer's price $12.50. Height 30 inches. Top 26x22, Legs 1⅝ inches square. One drawer 13x14x2½ inches deep. Shipping weight 70 pounds. Choice of Old Brass or Wood Drawer Knobs.

H354 Library Table

Come-Packt Price $7.75. Dealer's price $13.50. Height 30 inches. 36x36 inches round. Shipping weight 75 pounds.

H348 Library Table

Come-Packt Price $10.45. Dealer's price $14.50. Height 30 inches. Top 36x22 inches. One drawer 20x14x3 inches deep. Old Brass or Wood Drawer Knob. Shipping weight 120 pounds.

H352 Library Table

Come-Packt Price $13.45. Dealer's price $21.00. Height 30 inches. Top 44x28 inches. Legs 2½ inches square. 1 drawer 22x16x3 inches. Old Brass Drawer Pulls. Shipping weight 110 pounds.

H301 Library Table

Come-Packt Price $10.40. Dealer's price $18.50. Height 30 inches. Top 26x36 inches. Legs 2½ inches square. Shipping weight 95 pounds.

H353 Desk Table

Come-Packt Price $14.25. Dealer's price $22.50. Height 30 inches. Top 36x26 inches. Legs 1⅝ inches square. Two drawers 5⅞x5⅞x16 inches. Choice of Old Brass or Wood Drawer Knobs Shipping weight 135 pounds

H328 Elizabethan Library Table

Come-Packt Price $19.75. Dealer's price $55.00. Height 30 inches. Top 54x27 inches. Two drawers. Shipping weight 200 pounds.

H333 Flanders Library Table

Come-Packt Price $19.50. Dealer's price $48.00. Height 30 inches. Top 54x27 inches. Two drawers. Shipping weight 200 pounds.

H355 Den Table

Come-Packt Price $8.85. Dealer's price $15.50. Height 30 inches. Top 36x22 inches. Legs 1⅝ inches square. One drawer 20x16x3⅜ inches deep. Old Brass Drawer Pull. Shipping weight 85 pounds.

Buy Furniture Understandingly

The hardest problem of the young house-keeper is the selection of the furniture for the new home. Do not choose a "fad". It is often cheaply made and poorly finished and for the same amount of money you can buy Furniture of excellent design and of substantial worth, pleasing in outline and of a style that will not be a thing of the past in a few years. A few articles of unquestioned worth will give an effect that will be impossible to convey with a room full of furniture that cannot hide its inferiority.

H309 Library Table

Come-Packt Price $4.35. Dealer's price $7.75. Height 30 inches, top 27 inches, legs 1½ inches square. Shipping weight 65 pounds.

ASSEMBLED AND WELL PLEASED
The Library Table and Portieres ordered arrived. Have them assembled and am very much pleased with them. R. C. CLARK, Feb. 24, 1912.   R. F. D., Corning, Cal.

H311 Library Table

Come-Packt Price $10.45. Dealer's price $20.00. Without lower shelf, $9.00. Height 30 inches. Top 40 inches. Lower Shelf 19 inches. Legs 2½ inches square. Shipping weight 120 pounds.

H347 Library Table

Come-Packt Price $8.40. Dealer's price $14.00. Height 30 inches. Top 36x22 inches. Legs 1⅝ inches square. One drawer 21x16x3 inches. Shipping weight 80 pounds. Old Brass Drawer Pull.

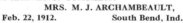

H367 Writing Table

Come-Packt Price $12.95. Dealer's price $19.50. Height 38½ inches. Top 22x36 inches. Legs 1¾ inches square. Four book shelves 18 inches long, 8½ inches deep, 9½ inches high. Choice of Old Brass or Wood Drawer Knob. Shipping weight 130 pounds.

Always mention the kind and color of cushion materials and finishes when ordering.

CAN'T SAY ENOUGH FOR IT
We received the goods in tip-top condition. Am certainly delighted. The table is a beauty. Really I can't say enough about it. Will continue to place orders with you until our entire house is furnished.

MRS. M. J. ARCHAMBEAULT,
Feb. 22, 1912.   South Bend, Ind.

H373 Library Table

Come-Packt Price $21.25. Dealer's price $29.50. Height 30 inches. Top 60x30 inches. Legs 2½ inches square. Two drawers, 4 book shelves, 22 inches long, 8 inches deep, 9 inches high. Choice of Old Brass or Wood Knobs. Shipping weight 230 pounds.

We own and operate our own factory, and the only steps between you and the rough lumber are our machine and packing rooms — there can never be any greater Economy than this.

H329 Library Table

Come-Packt Price $29.00. Dealer's price $60.00. Height 30 inches. Top 52x36 inches. Two drawers, (4 inches deep) on each side of table. Shipping weight 220 pounds.

"Ann Arbor" Mission Pianos and Player Pianos

Magnificent Instruments in Superb Come-Packt Cases at a Saving of $255 to $400

These splendid instruments combine the highest degree of musical and artistic excellence and afford the purchaser a direct saving of from $255 to $400.

The verdict of musical artists of the highest standing confirms our statement that they are absolutely unrivaled among pianos and player pianos selling below $750.

By special arrangement we have incorporated in our own exclusive designs of piano and player piano cases, the musical mechanism of one of the most celebrated makers in America.

The "Ann Arbor" Piano and Player Piano possesses the rich, harmonious, liquid tone, the sympathetic quality, clearness and sonority that distinguish the very highest grade of instruments regardless of name or price.

It is pre-eminently a perfect instrument, both in musical quality and structural soundness. The scale is flawless throughout its entire range.

Both as an instrument for playing accompaniments to the singing voice and for the interpretation of the most brilliant instrumental music, the "Ann Arbor" is from every standpoint supremely satisfactory.

BEAUTIFUL "COME-PACKT" DESIGNS

Our primary object in including pianos and player pianos with our other "Come-Packt" productions was to enable customers of ours to gratify their desires for complete harmony in music room or living room appointments.

The cases are quarter sawn white oak, in our exclusive designs, harmonizing perfectly with Come-Packt Furniture.

The purchaser, of course, has a choice of stains so that the finish will be identical with the balance of the furniture in the room.

Our master craftsmen have created for these matchless instruments cases of distinguished beauty, thoroughly in keeping with the most artistic environment. The cases are double laminated, both inside and out.

H63 Piano Seat

Come-Packt Price $7.50. Compartment under seat for sheet music. Height 21½ inches. Top 36x16 inches. Legs 1⅝ inches. Shipping weight 40 pounds. This seat included free with piano.

H442 Piano

Come-Packt Price $225.00. (Including Mission piano bench with compartments for music). Dealer's price $450.00. Furnished in quarter sawn white oak only and your choice of Mission finishes.

Price with interior player attachment, as shown in cut on opposite page $430.00. 88 note player furnished unless 65 note player is specified. Any piano player rolls may be used with this instrument.

Full seven and one-third Octaves; new and improved Grand Scale, smooth and even throughout; Overstrung Bass; Three Strings to a Note; Steel Bearing Bar; Convex Sounding Board; Double Repeating Action, with Nickel Brackets and Capstan Regulating Screws; Double Laminated Inside and Out; Rock Maple Laminated Wrest Plank, made up of seven pieces crossbanded; Solid Pilasters and Trusses; Three Pedals, Mouse Proof Patent Guard; Paneled Duet Swinging Music Desk; Boston Fall Board with Continuous Hinge; Best Quality of Ivory Keys and Solid Ebony Sharps; Full Composite Metal Plate.

Height, 4 feet 6½ inches. Width 5 feet 2 inches. Depth, 2 feet 3 inches.

Shipping weight 750 pounds.

H442 Piano

Come-Packt Piano Prices Save You Three Profits.

Piano manufacturers ordinarily figure $100 as the cost of selling a piano in the usual way, this amount representing the salaries, commissions and expenses of travelling salesmen. The wholesaler or jobber then adds his profit. On top of this comes the retail dealers' or agents' profits and all freights, handling and other expenses are also added to the selling price.

Our plan of selling furniture and pianos by mail direct from the factory to the user means the elimination of these three profits, great economy of freight and handling costs; does away with the necessity for expensive show rooms, salesmen's salaries and various other costs.

When you buy an "Ann Arbor" Come-Packt Piano or Player Piano, you pay for the actual cost of production, plus one small profit and you receive in return an absolutely high grade piano that is without a rival in the class below $750 in price.

Purchasers of our instruments have in every instance been more than pleased with the high quality and wonderful value. Each piano or player piano is strongly guaranteed and if not found exactly as represented and the best value obtainable for the money, we will take it back and refund every dollar of the purchase price and freight charges.

H442 Piano with entire front removed showing interior mechanism.

EVERY PURCHASER PLEASED

The Piano has arrived and is admired by all both for the quality of tone and finish. You certainly have the Prices Right for High Grade Goods.
A. P. Currier,
70 Blake Street, Lynn, Mass.

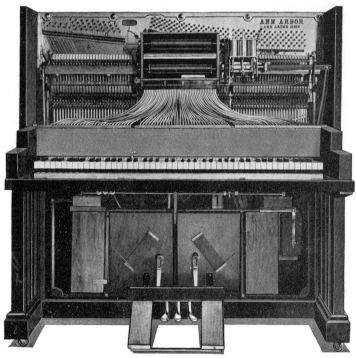

H442 Piano showing player mechanism with entire front removed. The mechanism is remarkably easy to operate and by manipulating the small keys and levers under the finger board the tone quality, tempo and expression can be modulated to interpret the mood or temperament of the artist.

"Built-in" Player Actions

Our piano player actions are mechanically perfect, the mechanism is "built-in" and a few simple movements will convert the piano into a player piano. The controlling devices afford a wide latitude of interpretation and responsiveness, only equalled by the most expensive player actions, and the untrained music lover has at his command the whole range of music from the popular ballad to the serious works of the Masters. The piano player is a perpetual delight to the whole household, and an appreciation of music may be attained in a short space of time that would otherwise require years of attendance at the opera or concert hall.

The player mechanism requires no sacrifice of the tone quality or appearance of the regulation piano, and when not in use as a player the piano gives little hint of its dual role. The player may be installed in our Mission case at the price shown under the description of the H442 piano on preceding page.

The pedals slip under the lower edge of the piano frame and do not mar the appearance of the front lower panel. Easy moving sliding panels in the upper movable front section permits the insertion of the music rolls when the piano is used with the playing mechanism. These small panels add to rather than detract from the splendid appearance of this mission design.

Quarter Sawn White Oak

HARMONIOUS AND ARTISTIC DINING ROOM FURNITURE

The prime essential of the well-appointed Dining Room is artistic furniture that harmonizes. Come-Packt Dining Room furniture affords a wide range of choice as to style of design.

Each set embodies separate and distinct characteristics, running all the way from the massive "Mission" type to the light and graceful "Sheraton."

Choose from among these varied styles that best expresses your individual taste and make your Dining Room "a feast for the eyes."

H471 Serving Table
Come-Packt Price $6.50. Dealer's price $10.50. Height 38 inches. Top 32x16 inches. Lower shelf 6 inches wide. Shipping weight 65 pounds.

THE FINISH YOU PREFER

The finish of COME-PACKT furniture is subdued in tone and color,—restful and pleasing.

Aside from the dollars-and-cents saving afforded by our furniture, there is the important advantage of being able to choose the particular color and tone in which your COME-PACKT Furniture shall be finished.

In buying from the miscellaneous stocks of furniture stores, one must be satisfied with such colors and tones as are offered.

The purchase of COME-PACKT furniture permits the buyer to express his or her *individuality* in the matter of color and tone.

Note the specimens of COME-PACKT *finishes,* both for wood and leather, shown on pages 73 and 74.

H124 Dining Chair
Come-Packt Price $3.25 each. (6) $18.95. Imperial leather covers, (1) Roan or Cowhide $3.65, (6) $20.90. With arms 75 cents each extra. Shipping weight (1) 45 pounds, (6) 160 pounds.

SPLENDID ADS FOR COME-PACKT

Furniture arrived in best of condition and we put all 9 pieces together in an evening. We take great pleasure in them and consider them splendid advertisements for your Company. Every article is superior to the idea we had from the illustrations, and are glad that you are branching out into other lines.

MRS. STUART B. SHAW,

May 1, 1911. Sisson, Calif.

H468 China Closet *Come-Packt Price $14.25* without glass. Dealer's price $22.50 (with glass inserted) $16.25. Height 61 ins. Top 27 x 14½ inches. Glass in door 40x18 inches. Ends 40x8 ins. Shipping weight 160 pounds. Mirror panel behind shelves, $1.50 each extra.

H125 Diner Chair
Come-Packt Price $3.45 each, (6) $19.75. Imperial leather covers. Roan or Cowhide (1) $3.95, (6) $22.70. With arms 75 cents each extra. Shipping weight (1) 45 pounds, (6) 160 pounds.

H470 Buffet
Come-Packt Price $22.30. An extremely neat little piece of dining room furniture, and while inexpensive it shows in every line its real quality and worth. One drawer lined with velour for silverware and the large drawer gives plenty of room for table-linen. The bevel plate mirror is 30 x 8 inches. Height 55 inches. Top 42x19 inches. Shipping weight 240 pounds. The dealer's price could hardly be less than $32.50.

All Dining Tables furnished with three plain sawn white oak leaves.

H372 Dining Table
Come-Packt Price $22.75, with 44-inch top. Retail value $36.50. (45-inch top), $23.75, (48-inch top), $25.75, (54-inch top), $28.00. Non-dividing pedestal and slides accommodate three 9-inch leaves only. Shipping weight (45-inch), 240 pounds. Choice of round or square top.

Quarter Sawn White Oak

THE SUPERIORITY OF WHITE OAK

White Oak is used exclusively in the manufacture of COME-PACKT Arts and Crafts, Mission and Flanders Furniture. It is very hard and strong, beautifully figured, uniform in color and under the manipulation of our master craftsmen takes on a fine, smooth surface.

The best examples of antique furniture are made from White Oak. It is the ideal cabinet wood and withstands all climatic conditions.

Its superiority over Red Oak is universally recognized.

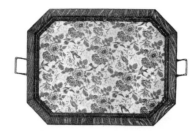

H434 Serving Tray
Come-Packt Price $4.75. Dealer's price $8.00. Size 24x18 inches. Brass handles. Plate glass over figured chintz. Shipping weight 40 pounds.

COME-PACKT DINING CHAIRS

In order that they may withstand the strain of constant service and much handling, COME-PACKT Dining Chairs, while light in weight, are made exceptionally strong and rigid. The seat rails, stretchers and back slats are carefully mortised and tenoned and all joints are tight and perfect fitting. They will stand the most severe tests. Our construction is accurate, scientific and painstaking.

H371 Dining Table
Come-Packt Price $22.25 with 44 inch top. Dealer's price $35.00, (45-inch) $23.25, (48-inch) $25.50, (54-inch) $27.75. Pedestal non-dividing slides, accommodate three 9-inch leaves only. Shipping weight (45-inch) 240 pounds. Choice of round or square top

H122 Diner
Come-Packt Price $3.45 each, (6) $19.75. Imperial leather covers. Roan or Cowhide (1), $4.15, (6) $24.75. Shipping weight (1) 45 pounds, (6) 160 pounds.

H317 Dining Table
Come-Packt Price $19.75. 45-inch. 48-inch top, $21.75. 54-inch top, $23.25. Dealer's price $36.00. Additional leaves (45-inch) 85 cents each. Height 30 inches. Legs 3¼ inches square. Will extend 7 feet 6 inches with 5 leaves. Three 9-inch leaves furnished. The prices include either round or square tops, and 3 leaves. Shipping weight (45-inch), 260 pounds.

H467 Buffet
One of the features of this design is the deep paneled doors, with arched tops and the mirror section with inverted pilasters. The large mirror, (38x10 inches), affords ample opportunity for the display of Cut Glass or China. One drawer is lined with velour. Height 57 inches. Top 48x20 inches. Shipping weight 290 pounds. A merchant would charge $50.00 for a buffet of equal quality. *Come-Packt Price $29.75.*

Buffets, Dressers, China Cabinets, and other "Case Goods" are shipped out completely assembled, except that one section will be left unfastened, thus securing the benefit of the lower freight rates.

H121 Diner
Come-Packt Price $3.60 each. (6) $19.95. Roan or Cowhide, (1) $4.15, (6) $24.95. Shipping weight (1) 45 pounds, (6) 160 pounds.

H465 China Closet
Come-Packt Price $19.25 without glass, retail value $32.50, (with glass inserted) $21.25. Solid dull brass trimmings. Glass in doors 38x11. Ends 38x8 inches. Shipping weight 190 pounds. Mirror panels behind shelves $2.75 each.

Quarter Sawn White Oak

Quality in Furniture

COME-PACKT Furniture combines extraordinary simplicity and beauty of design, materials of the highest grade and skilled workmanship in every detail.

Our furniture designs are **exclusive**; not mere copies of the "stock" patterns which one finds in every furniture store.

The solid, substantial construction of every piece of "COME-PACKT" furniture insures life-time satisfaction to the purchaser. It is built to last.

DELIVERED PRICES

If you cannot figure out the approximate price of our furniture delivered to your city from the freight table shown on page 72, do not hesitate to write to us. We will quote a delivered price to any place or port in the world.

H433 Serving Tray

Come-Packt Price $4.00. Dealer's price $7.50. Size 24x18, Brass Handles. Plate Glass over figured chintz. Shipping weight 40 pounds.

Our Service Department

If you are in doubt about the proper furniture for a particular room or for the entire house, or the color scheme for the different rooms, write to our **Service Department**; we will be glad to give you the benefit of our wide experience free of any charge whether you ultimately buy from us or not.

Allow five to six days for our finishing process. We take pride in our work and an indifferent finish will spoil the effect of the finest piece of furniture.

H120 Diner

Come-Packt Price $4.10 each. (6) $23.50. Roan skin or Cowhide (1) $5.35, (6) $31.00. Shipping weight (1) 45 pounds, (6) 160 pounds

H464 Buffet

A decidedly refined and handsome buffet, with an almost ideal arrangement of drawers and cupboards. The slight bevel around the edges of the drawers and the panel effect in the doors and the toilet, add the attractiveness of this splendid piece of furniture. Solid Dull Brass Trimmings, or wood knobs if preferred. The mirror is 30x10 inches. Height 57 inches. Top 54x21 inches. Shipping weight 325 pounds.

The usual price of this buffet is $55.00. **Come-Packt Price $30.85.**

H123 Diner

Come-Packt Price $3.95 each. (6) $22.75. Imperial leather covers, Roan or Cowhide, (1) $5.25 each, (6) $30.50. Shipping weight (1) 45 pounds, (6) 160 pounds.

H365 Dining Table

Come-Packt Price $27.75, with 48-inch top. Dealer's price $43.50. (45-inch top), $23.25. (54-inch top), $29.50. (60-inch top), $31.50. Prices include round or square top and 3 leaves with pedestal and top lock. Slides will accommodate 6 nine inch leaves. Shipping weight (48-inch), 325 pounds, (54-inch), 365 pounds.

H344 Dining Table

Come-Packt Price $22.50. 48-in. top. With 54-in. top, $24.00. Dealer's price $45.00. Height 30 in., Legs 3¼ in. square, will extend to 9 feet with 6 leaves. Three plain oak 9-in. leaves only furnished; extra leaves 54-inch, $1.00 each. Shipping weight, 54-inch, 300 pounds.

All Pieces on This Page Solid Quarter Sawn White Oak.

Make up a list of pieces you are interested in and ask us for a price with freight added to your city.

H100 Diner

Come-Packt Price $2.75. Six $16.00. Imperial leather seat pad. Dealer's price $4.50 each. Cowhide or Roan skin, 50 cents each extra. Height 38 inches, Seat 17½x18 inches. Shipping weight 50 pounds, six 160 pounds.

H413 Buffet

Come-Packt Price $19.75. Dealer's price $40.00. Height 47 inches. Width 48 inches. Depth, 20 inches. Legs 1⅝ inches. Height to top shelf 40 inches. Four drawers, Old Brass Trimmings. Shipping weight 270 pounds.

H385 Pedestal Table

Come-Packt Price $27.25. (54-inch top). With 60-inch Top, $29.75; with 48-inch Top, $24.75, with 45-inch Top, $24.75. Dealer's price $47.00. Height 30 inches, Top will extend to 9 feet with six leaves; three 9-inch leaves only furnished, extra leaves 54-inch $1.00. Top and pedestal lock included. Shipping weight, 54-inch, 370 pounds. These prices include round or square top and 3 plain oak leaves.

H112 Diner

Come-Packt Price $5.50. Six $31.50. Imperial leather cushions. Dealer's price $9.00 each. Cowhide or Roan skin Covers, $2.75 each extra. With arms 75 cents extra per chair. Height 38 inches, Seat 17½x18 inches. These chairs cannot be shipped in sections. The above prices include cost of assembling and packing. Shipping weight 50 pounds; six, 180 pounds. Spring seat cushions furnished with H112 chairs.

H427 Buffet

Come-Packt Price $29.25. With French bevel plate mirror. Dealer's price $60.00. Height 55 inches, Height to top shelf 40 inches, Width 56 inches, Depth 21 inches, Legs 2¼ inches, Mirror 10x44 inches. Three drawers, Old Brass Trimmings. Shipping weight 330 pounds.

Arms for all diners will be furnished for 75 cents net extra per chair. Add 75 cents to the price for six chairs if one of the set is to be furnished with arms as shown in illustration above.

H429 Buffet

Come-Packt Price $21.25. Dealer's price $42.00. Bevel French Mirror. Height 57 inches, Height to top shelf 40 inches, Width 48 inches, Depth 20 inches, Legs 1⅝ inches, Mirror 10x30 inches. Four drawers, Old Brass Trimmings. Shipping weight 280 pounds.

H346 Serving Table

Come-Packt Price $8.75. Dealer's price $15.00. Height 34½ inches, Top 35x18 inches. Shipping weight 125 pounds.

H428 China Closet

Come-Packt Price $17.75. (Including mirror but not glass). Glass inserted, $2.50 extra. Dealer's price $42.00. Height 59 inches, Width 36 inches, Depth 16 inches, Mirror 6x24 inches, Glass 14x26 inches and 10x26 inches. Shipping weight 220 pounds.

Quarter Sawn White Oak

HOW TO CARE FOR FURNITURE

The life and beauty of the finish on a piece of furniture depends to a large extent on the treatment it receives.

It is best never to use soap and water on any piece of furniture that has been schellaced, varnished or waxed. Some furniture will stand this method of keeping it bright but as a vast majority will not, it is best not to use soap or water on any of them.

Use a good reliable furniture polish only. They will remove the dirt, and leave enough oil on the surface to give new life and lustre to the finish. Polish with a piece of cheese cloth.

Enameled Furniture of the better grades may be washed with soapy water and then polished with a reliable furniture polish.

Mission or waxed surfaces should be rubbed up two or three times a year with a cloth dampened in liquid wax after which it

H469 Serving Table
Come-Packt Price $10.50. Retail value $17.50. Height 41 inches. Top 36x18½ inches. Lower shelf 7½ inches wide. Posts 1⅝ inches square. Shipping weight 85 pounds.

may be brought to a lustre by polishing with a dry cheese cloth. Never use the ordinary furniture polish on a waxed surface.

Gold furniture should be only wiped off with a soft dry chamois.

The less brass beds are rubbed, the longer the finish will last. Use a soft sponge and soapy water sparingly. Dry at once with a soft chamois.

Clean mirrors and glasses with a mixture of water, ammonia and whiting, and rub with cheese cloth.

Leathers are susceptible to climatic changes and the condition of the leather and the life of it depends somewhat on the care it receives. An occasional wiping with sweet oil is the best preservative. Keep leather covers out of the sun as much as possible and remember that deterioration goes on even more rapidly when not in use than when used with proper care.

H126 Diner Chair
Come-Packt Price $3.50 each. (6) $20.00. Imperial leather covers. Cowhide or Roan skin, $3.95 each. (6) $23.75. With arms 75 cents per chair extra. Height 38 inches. Shipping weight (1) 45 pounds, (6) 160 pounds.

H369 Dining Table
Come-Packt Price $28.75. 48-inch top. Retail value $45.00. (45-inch top) $24.95. (54-inch top) $29.75. (60-inch top) $32.50. Choice of round or square tops. Three plain oak leaves furnished and pedestal and top locks. Slides will accommodate 6 leaves. Shipping weight (48-inch) 325 pounds. (54-inch) 365 pounds.

H118 Diner Chair
Come-Packt Price $4.15 each. (6) $23.75. Imperial leather covers. Cowhide or Roan skin $5.35 each, (6) $31.00. With arms 75 cents per chair extra. Height 38 inches. Shipping weight (1) 45 pounds, (6) 160 pounds.

H462 Buffet
The severe simplicity of this buffet appeals to those who are looking for a pure Mission design. The absence of ornamentation of any kind, the plain square wood knobs, the massive proportions and quiet dignity is in pleasing contrast with many of the carved and highly polished buffets that are entirely out of place in a mission dining room.

There is ample room in the long drawer for linen and the compartments below are large and roomy. One drawer is lined with velour for silver. The beveled mirror is 38x10 inches. Height 5 inches. Top 56x21 inches. Shipping weight 330 pounds. A reasonable price for this buffet would be $60.00. Come-Packt Price $43.85.

H463 China Closet
Come-Packt Price $23.50, without glass. Retail value $35.00. (With glass), $25.50. Height 64 inches. Top 40x15½ inches. Solid Brass Trimmings. Large glass in doors 38x12 inches. Glass in sides 37x8 inches. Shipping weight 220 pounds. Mirror panels behind shelves $3.30 each.

Quarter Sawn White Oak

Direct from Factory to You—Save Half

The reason that *Come-Packt* can be sold at *about half* the ordinary store price is that the entire output of our factories goes *direct* from our finishing rooms *to your home.* All the usual selling expenses, salesmen's commissions and expenses, dealer's profits, store expenses, credit losses, the inefficiency of the old way of doing business; high freight rates, expensive packing—ALL are eliminated by buying direct from our factory.

Consider for a moment the statements we have made. Everyone knows them to be indisputable and if the saving of money is any consideration to *you,* send to-day for the designs that will harmonize with your interiors or with the rest of your furniture. Your choice of eight different stains will enable you to follow out color schemes that would be *impossible* under any other plan.

Do not make the mistake of thinking that *Come-Packt* Furniture is not an economy to the city buyer; the larger the city the heavier the ordinary selling expenses and costs of doing business. You will find *Come-Packt* Furniture in the well-appointed homes in New York and in the modest home of the small village, but no matter where you live, *Come-Packt* will give you 100 cents *worth of real value* for *every dollar spent* and more than a life-time of *satisfactory service.*

H318 Tea-Table

Come-Packt Price $4.25.
Dealer's price $8.00.
Height 28½ inches. Top 19x11½
inches. Shipping weight 80 pounds.

A Remarkable Sales Plan for Remarkable Furniture

Several factories make *Come-Packt* Sectional Furniture the best value your money can buy, regardless of price.

Refinement of detail and correct design are vital parts of the *Come-Packt* business. The choicest *Quarter Sawn White Oak* is used throughout—this fact alone indicates the quality of our furniture. The handsome mission pieces are the creation of a practical designer. Every piece is exclusive with us and can be purchased *nowhere else.* The construction is solid and substantial, yet every piece is well-proportioned and dignified in appearance—no structural details have been slighted or neglected that could in any way add to the attractiveness or quality of the furniture.

The thorough sincerity of *Come-Packt* Furniture will be apparent when you receive it—every part may be readily inspected; there is no chance to conceal defects—no possibility of covering up incompetent workmanship or slighted details. You need not be a furniture expert to realize that it is *honest all through,* and regardless of price *no* furniture can surpass *Come-Packt* in real *merit* and artistic *worth.*

H370 Dining Table

Come-Packt Price $27.50. With 48-inch top. Retail value $45.00. (54-inch top), $29.90. (60-inch top), $32.50. Prices include either round or square top, pedestal and top locks and three 9-inch oak leaves. Slides will accommodate 6 leaves. Extra leaves (48-inch) 90 cents each, (54-inch) $1.00 each, (60-inch) $1.10. Shipping weight (48-inch) 325 pounds, (54-inch) 365 pounds.

H466 Serving Table

Come-Packt Price $10.50. Retail value $17.50. Height 41 inches. Top 36x18½ inches. Shipping weight 85 pounds.

H460 Buffet

This fine piece is made of solid Quarter Sawn White Oak and the effect of the high side doors and broad mirror, (44x10) makes this a massive appearing buffet especially suited for paneled beamed ceilings and paneled side walls. Each compartment has a wide shelf for dishes or linen and one drawer is lined with velour for silver. Solid dull brass trimmings, or wood knobs if preferred. Height 57 inches. Top 58x22½ inches. Shipping weight 350 pounds. The retail price of this buffet is $70.00 Come-Packt Price $49.75.

H461 China Closet

Come-Packt Price $21.83 without glass. Dealer's price $32.50. (with glass inserted), $23.75. Height 64 inches. Top 40x15 inches. Glass in doors 38x12 inches. Glass in ends 37x8 inches. Shipping weight 220 pounds. Mirror panels behind shelves, $2.90 each, extra.

Quarter Sawn White Oak

FURNITURE VALUES

If every purchaser of Furniture was informed as to furniture values and the cost and qualities of the materials ordinarily used in making furniture, it would be a waste of time to put more than our selling prices below each design shown in this book, but because so few people really know what constitutes a dollar's worth of value in furniture we give, in this catalog, some of the points to be considered in buying furniture so that you will be informed as to what constitutes quality in furniture and can judge for yourself, whether you buy from us or others, as to the ratio between PRICE and VALUE.

H459 Serving Table

Come-Packt Price $12.69. Retail value $19.50. Height 44 in. Top 40x20 inches. Drawer 24x14x3 inches. Solid Brass Trimmings. Shipping weight 125 pounds.

FINE FURNITURE

You know it the minute you see it, it needs no recommendation and calls for no apology. We cannot show the quality of materials in a photograph, but we have the confidence in our goods to back them with a guarantee of satisfaction that means all that we could wish a guarantee to mean if we were buying furniture instead of selling it.

The pre-eminence of the COME-PACKT FURNITURE COMPANY is due to the high standard that we have maintained in our merchandising policy,—to the liberality and fairness with which we treat all purchasers and to the undisputed worthiness of our products.

H118 Diner Chair (with arms)

Come-Packt Price $4.90 each. (6) $28.40. Imperial leather covers Cowhide or Roan skin $6.10 each, (6) $35.50. Shipping weight (1) 45 pounds, (6) 160 pounds.

H364 Dining Table

Come-Packt Price $28.75, 48-inch top. Retail value $45.00, (45-inch top) $25.25, (54-inch top) $30.50, (60-inch top) $33.00. Round or square top and 3 leaves. Pedestal and top lock included. Slides will accommodate six 9-inch leaves. Shipping weight, (48-inch) 325 pounds, (54-inch) 365 pounds.

H119 Diner Chair

Come-Packt Price $4.25 each. (6) $25.50. Imperial leather covers. Cowhide or Roan skin $5.40 each, (6) $31.25. With arms 75 cents per chair extra. Shipping weight (1) 45 pounds, (6) 160 pounds.

H458 China Closet

Come-Packt Price $33.25, without glass. Retail value $48.00. With glass inserted $35.75. Height 62 in., top 51x15 in. Solid brass trimmings. Glass in door 38x18 in., side 38x10 in., ends 38x8 in. Shipping weight 270 pounds. Mirror panels behind shelves $4.45 each.

H457 Buffet

A handsome design of unusual merit and attractiveness, and as in all Come-Packt designs, the correct proportions considerably enhance the artistic appearance of this splendid design. The middle drawer is wide and deep being 47x17½x7 inches and gives ample room for table linen. One top drawer is lined with velour and divided into three compartments for silver. The trimmings are dull brass, or if desired, wood knobs will be furnished. The beveled French plate mirror is 10x44 inches. The top is of solid Oak and 60x22½ inches. The retail price of a buffet of equal merit would be $75.00. *Come-Packt Price $55.00.* Shipping weight 350 pounds.

Quarter-Sawn White Oak

Flanders Dining Room Suit

H106 Arm Diner

Come-Packt Price $7.00. (Imperial leather cushions.) ½ doz. chairs (Imperial leather) $40.00. Cow hide cover, $2.00 each extra. Roan skin, $2.50 extra. Dealer's price $14.25. Height 41½ inches. Shipping weight (1) 50 pounds, (6) 220 pounds.

H326 Serving Table

Come-Packt Price $7.50. Dealer's price $14.75. Height 33 inches. Top 35x18 inches. Shipping weight 85 pounds.

H105 Diner

Come-Packt Price $5.50. (Imperial leather cushion). ½ dozen chairs (Imperial leather) $31.50. Cowhide cover, $1.50 each extra. Roan skin, $2.00 extra. Dealer's price $12.25. Height 41½ inches. Shipping weight (1) 50 pounds, (6) 190 pounds.

H110 Arm Diner

Come-Packt Price $8.00. (Imperial leather cushion.) ½ dozen chairs (Imperial leather) $48.50. Cowhide Cover, $2.50 each extra. Roan skin, $3.00 extra. Dealer's price $15.50. Height 41½ inches. Shipping weight (1) 55 pounds, (6) 210 pounds.

H325 Dining Table

Come-Packt Price $29.75. (54-inch top) 60 inch top, $34.50. Extra leaves, $1.00 each, 54 inch. Dealer's price $65.00. Height 30 inches. Will extend to 9 feet with 6 leaves. Three 9-inch leaves furnished. Prices include either round or square top and 3 plain sawn white oak leaves.

H109 Diner

Come-Packt Price $6.50. (Imperial leather cushion.) ½ dozen chairs (Imperial leather) $37.50. Cowhide Cover, $2.00 each extra. Roan skin, $2.50 extra. Dealer's price $13.50. Height 41½ inches. Shipping weight (1) 55 pounds, (6) 210 pounds.

WORTH THREE TIMES ITS COST

I can best express my appreciation and delight with my dining room suite by saying that I would not sell it for three times the amount I paid for it.

LOUIS J. BRAUN

Sept. 29, 1911.   5 Ryan St., Buffalo, N. Y.

We guarantee safe arrival of goods at destination. The quality of materials and workmanship warrants our unusual guarantee of satisfaction or money refunded.

H422 China Closet (with mirror)

Come-Packt Price $19.75. (Including mirror but not glass.) With glass, $21.75. Dealer's price $40.00. Height 60½ inches. Width 37 inches. Depth 16 inches. Mirror 6x24 inches. Glass in doors, 14x26 inches. Glass in sides, 10x26 inches. Shipping weight 220 pounds.

H327 Serving Table

Come-Packt Price $9.75. Dealer's price $19.50. Height 33 inches, top 35x18 inches. Shipping weight 130 pounds.

H421 Buffet (with mirrors)

Come-Packt Price $34.75. Dealer's price $70.00. Extreme height 51 inches. Height to top shelf 40 inches. Width 56 inches. Depth 21¼ inches. (2) mirrors 6x20 inches Shipping weight 330 pounds.

The designs on this page are offered in either the Quarter Sawn White Oak with any of the mission finishes; or Quartered Satin Walnut with either the Mahogany or Circassian Walnut varnish finish, at 10% extra.

The designs on this page are offered in either the Quarter Sawn White Oak with any of the mission finishes; or Quartered Satin Walnut with either the Mahogany or Circassian Walnut varnish finish, at 10% extra.

H116 Diner

Come-Packt Price $4.75. Six $27.00. Dealer's price $10.00 each. Height 39 inches, Seat 17x17. Imperial leather. Cowhide or Roan skin 65 cents extra each. Shipping weight (1) 30 pounds, (6) 120 pounds.

H448 China Closet

Come-Packt Price $19.25. (Without glass or mirror). Dealer's price $45.00. Height 59 inches, top 36x17½, posts 1½ inches square, glass inserted $2.50 extra. Mirror 28x18; $3.50 extra. Glass shelves furnished for $2.50 each extra. Glass in sides, 37x9, glass in doors 37x11 inches. Shipping weight 230 pounds.

H117 Arm Diner

Come-Packt Price $6.75. Six $39.00. Dealer's price $12.50 each. Height 39 inches, Seat 19x19¼ inches. Imperial leather. Cowhide 75 cents each extra. Shipping weight (1) 35 pounds, (6) 140 pounds.

H114 Diner

Come-Packt Price $5.25. Dealer's price $9.00, six $30.00. Height 39 inches, seat 17x17 inches. Imperial leather. Cow hide or Roan skin 65 cents each extra. Shipping weight (1) 30 pounds, (6) 120 pounds.

H362 Pedestal Table

Come-Packt Price $29.75. Dealer's price $65.00. (54-inch top). With 60-inch top $34.50. With 48-inch top $26.50. Height 30 inches. Top will extend to 9 feet with 6 leaves, 3 plain sawn leaves only furnished, extra leaves 54 inch, $1.00 each. Top and pedestal lock included. Shipping weight 54 inches, 360 pounds.

H115 Arm Diner

Come-Packt Price $7.25. Six, $42.00. Dealer's price $12.00 each. Height 39 inches, Seat 19 x 19¼. Imperial leather. Cowhide or Roan skin 75 cents extra. Shipping weight (1) 35 pounds, (6) 140 pounds.

H360 Serving Table

Come-Packt Price $10.75. Dealer's price $21.00. Height 35 inches. Top 39x20 inches. Legs 1⅝ inch square. Two drawers 15 x 15 x 3½ inches deep. Shipping weight 90 pounds.

H361 Serving Table

Come-Packt Price $8.50. Dealer's price $17.00. Height 35 inches, top 36 x 19 inches, lower shelf 32 x 14 inches. Shipping weight 75 pounds.

H444 Buffet

Come-Packt Price $36.75. Dealer's price $70.00. Extreme height 55 inches. To top 40½ inches. Size of top 58x21, posts 2¼ inches square, mirror 44x10 inches. 1 drawer lined with velour for silver and furnished with Yale lock. Shipping weight 330 pounds.

Quarter Sawn White Oak

ISN'T IT REASONABLE

To suppose that a Concern that has conducted from the start an increasingly successful business has done so by studying and catering to the demands of an exacting public? Our success has been attained only by giving the high quality that we claimed for our products and by an unswerving policy of dealing with others as we would be done by.

We are jealous of our reputation for clean merchandising. We have spent years in building up this high reputation for good goods, splendid values and fair dealing, and we guard this reputation as the most valuable asset of an extraordinary business success.

H646 Ladies' Dressing Table
Come-Packt Price $12.75. (Including French Bevel Plate Mirror). Dealer's price $19.50, Height to case top 30 inches, Top 32 in. by 19 in. Mirror 20x16 in. Shipping weight 110 pounds.

WHO MAKES IT—WHO STANDS BACK OF ITS QUALITY?

That's the question that interests you as a buyer of any kind of Goods,—don't be afraid to ask that question of any Concern you buy from. If they evade the question,—buy elsewhere.

Buy Furniture from the view point of service, and above all, buy from a Concern that thinks highly enough of its own products to give them a name that they are willing to back up in every detail. Compare our products with those of any other Concern, but compare QUALITY first and then the price. You'll like COME-PACKT in your home.

H12 Nursery Rocker
Come-Packt Price $5.50. Dealer's price $8.25. Imperial leather auto-spring cushion. Cowhide Cover, $7.25. Roan skin $6.75. Height 32 inches. Seat 16½x16½ inches. Shipping weight 65 pounds.

H619 Bed
Come-Packt Price $14.00. (Single bed 3 feet 6 inches wide $12.25). Dealer's price $28.50. Height head 49 inches, Foot 42½ inches, Length 6 feet 6 inches, Width 4 feet 6 inches, Posts 2¼ inches. Shipping weight, 170 pounds, Shipping weight, single bed, 135 pounds.

H31 Slipper Chair
Come-Packt Price $5.25. Dealer's price $8.00. Imperial leather auto-spring cushions. Cowhide Covers $6.95. Roan skin $6.75. Height 34 inches, Seat 16½x 16½ inches. Shipping weight 65 pounds.

H643 Cheval Glass
Come-Packt Price $17.25. With French Bevel Plate Mirror. Dealer's price $26.50. Extreme height 67 inches, Width 26 inches, Mirror 48x18 inches. Shipping weight 110 pounds.

H628 Bed
Come-Packt Price $16.25. Full width 4 feet 6 inches. Dealer's price $32.00. (Single bed 3 feet 6 inches wide $14.65). All beds are 6 feet 6 inches long. Height (head) 49 inches, (Foot) 39 inches. Shipping weight 140 pounds. Our springs and mattresses fit these beds perfectly. Order a complete outfit to be shipped to you.

H629 Cheval Glass
Come-Packt Price $16.50. (Including French Beve Plate Mirror). Dealer's price $25.00. Extreme height 70 inches, Width 26 inches, Mirror 48x 18 inches. Shipping weight 110 pounds.

Solid Quarter Sawn White Oak

The unusual charm of these pure Mission pieces in the best of selected Quartered White Oak is due partly to the cleverness of the design itself,—the tenons of the lock rails protrude through the posts and give an artistic craftsman appearance that is particularly pleasing in a Mission Bed room. A filled and hand rubbed varnish finish will be applied to any of the Mission designs for 10 per cent extra. Allow not less than ten to fourteen days for the rubbed finish as good work cannot be done in less time.

Dull rubbed or polished varnish finish on mission designs 10 per cent. extra.

Many manufacturers, usually of the Nameless kind, will tell you that "Oak is Oak." An article may be truly sold as "Solid Oak" and yet be built of inferior Oak. The first requisite is the selection of thoroughly seasoned and kiln-dried lumber of high grade. Quarter Sawn Oak, owing to the great waste in its manufacture, costs nearly twice as much as the plain sawn oak. White Oak is the best of many different varieties of oak.

We do not urge you to buy from us if we can show you no economy in the transaction, but a comparison of qualities will show that our prices offer you a considerable saving in the cost of your furniture.

H614 Ladies' Dressing Table

Come-Packt Price $10.75. (Including French bevel plate mirror). Dealer's price $19.00. Extreme height 57 inches, Height to top shelf 30 inches, Top 34x18½ inches, Mirror 20x18 inches. Shipping weight 130 pounds.

H660 Dresser

Come-Packt Price $19.75. (Including French bevel plate mirror). Dealer's price $28.50. Extreme height 70 inches, Height to top shelf 34 inches, Width 39 inches, Depth 19 inches, Mirror 24x30 inches. Shipping weight 200 pounds.

H604 Wash Stand

Come-Packt Price $7.75. Dealer's price $11.00. Extreme height 48½ inches, Height to top shelf 30 inches, Width 34 inches, Depth 18¼ inches. Shipping weight 100 pounds.

H610 Princess Dresser

Come-Packt Price $18.75. (Including French bevel plate mirror). Dealer's price $30.00. Extreme height 71 inches, Height to top shelf 26 inches, Width 39½ inches, Depth 19 inches. Mirror 20x36 inches. Shipping weight 210 pounds.

H632 Highboy

Come-Packt Price $20.75. (Including French bevel plate mirror). Without mirror $18.50. Dealer's price $34.50. Extreme height 76 inches, Height to top shelf 50 inches, Width 33½ inches, Depth 18¼ inches, Mirror 18x20 inches. Shipping weight 235 pounds.

H631 Cheval Glass

Come-Packt Price $15.75. (Including French bevel plate mirror). Dealer's price $24.00. Extreme height 69 inches, Width 28 inches, Mirror 18x50 inches. Shipping weight 110 pounds.

Quarter Sawn White Oak

A Passing Sensation

COME-PACKT FURNITURE is passing from the stage of a *sensation* into that of an *institution.*

Sensations are usually built on shifting sands and the sensation of today is discarded or forgotten tomorrow. COME-PACKT is founded on the enduring rock of *service,* the corner-stone is QUALITY and it is built on HONOR. The structure is worthy of your confidence and patronage.

The hairy Hubbard of East Aurora has said: "We make our living from our friends," and it's true because our enemies never buy from us. We treat every buyer as a friend and retain him or her as a friend after each transaction,—you'll appreciate this better after buying COME-PACKT.

Specify color of cushion materials and stains when ordering. All Mission and Bungalow furniture will be shipped finished unless otherwise ordered.

More Value for Your Furniture Dollars

B. F. Yokum, Chairman of the St. Louis & San Francisco Railroad, figures that Consumers pay thirteen billion dollars for food that the farmer sells for six billion. The Transportation Companies and Middlemen get one billion more than the Farmer himself gets for it.

The Furniture business of the Country amounts to only three hundred million dollars but of this amount it is estimated that the manufacturer receives less than one half,—What is the answer? Buy DIRECT from the Manufacturer and GET MORE VALUE FOR YOUR FURNITURE DOLLARS. (i.e., buy COME-PACKT).

H645 High Boy

H642 Ladies' Dressing Table

H647 Wash Stand

Come-Packt Price $8.25. Dealer's Price $13.50. Height 31 inches. Top 32x19 inches. Posts 1¾ inches. Shipping weight 70 pounds. Shipped in sections.

Come-Packt Price $22.85. (Including French Bevel Mirror.) Dealer's price $36.00. Extreme height 76 inches. Top 32x20 inches. Height to top of case 51 inches, Mirror 20x16 inches. Shipping weight 205 pounds.

Come-Packt Price $16.25. (Including French Bevel Plate Mirror.) Dealer's price $27.00. Extreme height 53 inches, Top 40x20 inches. Height to top of case 29 inches. Shipping weight 120 pounds. Mirror 26x18 inches.

Order a Come-Packt Spring and Mattress to go with the Bed Room Furniture.

See page 73 for description of finishes.

Do not confuse the words "Price" and "Value." "Price" is always arbitrary, while "Value" is inherent in the goods and entirely independent of the price.

H644 Dresser

H627 Bed

Come-Packt Price $16.95. (Full width 54 inches). Dealer's price $35.00. Height (head), 50 inches. Foot 37 inches. Length 6 feet 6 inches. (Single bed 3 feet 6 inches wide $15.45). Shipping weight full size 140 pounds—single 135 pounds. All beds accommodate a 6 foot 2 inch mattress and a regulation size spring.

Come-Packt Price $24.60. With French Bevel Plate Mirror 26x30 inches. Extreme height 65 inches. Height of case 35 inches. Top 42x20 inches. Shipping weight 200 pounds. Lock and keys furnished with all dressers and highboys.

QUARTER-SAWN WHITE OAK IS USED EXCLUSIVELY unless other materials are mentioned in the description under each piece.

Plain, Simple, Substantial

I am quite proud of the furniture purchased of you and it is much admired by my friends. The Brown Flemish finish harmonizes perfectly with my walls and woodwork and the styles could not be improved on,—so plain, simple and substantial without being severe.

Mrs. Louise B. Kilbourne,
849 Lewis Ave.

June 8, 1912.
St. Joseph, Mich

H620 Shirt Waist Box

Come-Packt Price $9.25. Dealer's price $17.50. Height 22 inches, top 30 x 18, posts 1⅝ inches square, 4 drawers 23 long x 13½ x 2⅜ inches deep. Old Brass Drawer Pulls. Convenient drawers for waists or lingerie. Shipping weight 110 pounds

H623 Ladies' Dressing Table

Come-Packt Price $12.75. Dealer's price $22.00. Height 54 inches, to top shelf 31½ inches. Top 36 x 18, posts 1⅝ inches square. 2 drawers 13 by 12x3¾ inches deep. Old Brass Drawer Pulls. Shipping weight 130 pounds.

The **Dresser Chair No. 32** is a splendid companion piece for this dressing table H623.

H622 Highboy

Come-Packt Price $24.50. Dealer's price $44.50. Extreme height 73 inches, top 36 x 18, posts 1⅝ inches square. Mirror 24x18 inches. (Without mirror $22.75.) Door space 13½x10¾x 16 inches deep. Lock on top drawer. Old Brass Drawer Pulls. Shipping weight 245 pounds.

H624 Wash Stand

Come-Packt Price $7.75. Dealer's price $14.00. Height 31½ inches, top 36 x 18, posts 1⅝ inches square. Shipping weight 100 pounds.

H32 Desk or Dresser Chair
Come-Packt Price $4.75. Dealer's price $9.50. Height 32½ inches, Legs 1¾ inches. This chair is a companion piece for the ladies' desks or it may be used as a ladies' dressing table chair. Shipping weight 50 pounds.

You are certain of the right quality and sure of the right price when you buy "Come-Packt."

REFER TO THE INDEX ON PAGE SIX WHEN OTHER DESIGN NUMBERS ARE MENTIONED.

H681 Cane Panel Bed

Come-Packt Price $16.75. (Single bed 3 feet 6 inches wide $14.75). Dealer's price $30.00. Height (head) 49 inches, foot 42½ inches. Length 6 feet 6 inches, width 4 feet 6 inches. Shipping weight 165 pounds. Shipping weight single bed, 130 pounds. This bed will be finished in white enamel at $24.50 full size

H621 Dresser

Come-Packt Price $26.75. Dealer's price $45.00. Extreme height 69 inches, to top shelf 34½ inches, top 46x20, posts 1⅝ inches square. Two top drawers 18x15½x4½ inches deep, fitted with locks. Middle drawer 6½ inches deep, bottom drawer 7¼x40x15½ inches. Mirror 34x28 inches. Shipping weight 245 pounds.

Quartered White Oak

Quality Counts

It's the Quality and not the Type, Design or Price that determines the life, or wear of Furniture.

There are a great many different qualities in OAK ranging from a coarse fibred, porous, brashy texture up to the beautifully figured hard and smooth grained quarter sawn white oak such as used in COME-PACKT Furniture. A better quality of oak has never been grown than we use, and QUALITY COUNTS.

Mission and Bungalow furniture will be shipped stained and finished unless your order specifies "unstained."

A Comfortable Day Begins the Night Before

You'll never know what it means to you the day after until you have started right by getting into a bed that is a real bed the night before,—(A real bed has comfortable springs and mattresses that give a sense of suspension, of being buoyed up on all sides with an equal pressure on every outline, angle, hump or hollow). And we have provided comfortable days for you by offering beds, springs and mattresses that start the day right for you,— the night before. COME-PACKT Service and Quality await your commands.

HIGH-BOY A BEAUTY

The High-Boy dresser received some time ago and must say that it is a beauty. Am well satisfied and I hope to be able to order some more pieces later on. Yours truly,

J. B. KORSTAD,

Aug. 3d, '10.   Gooding, Idaho

H641 Ladies' Dressing Table

Come-Packt Price $18.25 with three plain plate mirrors. (Note: bevel mirrors would be unsatisfactory in these frames on account of the reflecting surfaces). Dealer's price $35.00. Extreme height 50 inches, Height to top of case 29 inches, Top 40x20 inches. Shipping weight 115 pounds. Shipped in sections.

H640 High Boy

Come-Packt Price $33.25. Including French Bevel Plate Mirror, size 26x18 inches. Dealer's Price $50.00, Extreme height 76 inches, Height to top of case 52 inches, Top 40x22 inches. The lower cupboard provides ample room for shoes or other bulky articles. Shipping weight 240 pounds.

H59 Dressing Table Chair

Come-Packt Price $4.75. Dealer's price $9.50. Height of seat 18 inches, Extreme height 30 inches. This chair will harmonize perfectly with any of our bedroom suites. Shipping weight 35 pounds

H639 Dresser

Come-Packt Price $38.65. With French Bevel Plate Mirror size 42½x30 inches. Dealer's price $55.00. Top 24x52, Height of case 35 inches, Extreme height 71 inches. Shipping weight 245 pounds.

Quarter Sawn White Oak used exclusively unless otherwise mentioned in the description of each piece.

H638 Bed

Come-Packt Price $16.95. Dealer's price $35.00. Full width (4 feet 6 inches), Height of head 47 inches, Foot 38 inches. Single Bed 3 feet 6 inches $15.25). Shipping weight (4 feet 6 inches) 140 pounds.

White Enamel Bedroom Suite

Every finish that looks white is not White Enamel. The genuine White Enamel finish that we use is a long and expensive process (it takes 20 days to complete the finish) but when completed, no better White Enamel finish can be produced. Six coats are applied and each one sanded and rubbed and the last coat is polished to a beautiful lustrous surface. This surface may be washed without damaging it,—use soapy water (only) and polish with a chamois or soft cloth.

The COME-PACKT Trade-Mark is back of every article sold by this Company,—The Trade-Mark identifies the quality and the maker and our Guarantee is the Bond of Good Faith that we give with each purchase.

Read what one of the brightest advertising minds of America said in his weekly letter to advertisers in Collier's Weekly of Mar. 16th, 1912:

"When you choose merchandise bearing a familiar trade-mark, you have actual assurance of quality, for the trade-mark identifies the manufacturer who thus must stand full responsibility for the quality of his goods. He expects to sell you again and again or he would not use a trade-mark."

Signed,
E. C. Patterson,
Manager Adverting Department

H637 Ladies' Dressing Table

Come-Packt Price $17.50, Retail value $30.00. Extreme height 55 inches, Height to top of case 30 inches, Top 30x19 inches, Mirror 20x18 inches. Shipping weight 120 pounds.

H648 Wash Stand
Come-Packt Price $12.95. (Same as H637 Ladies' Dressing Table without Mirror).

H636 Highboy

Come-Packt Price $34.50. Dealer's price $50.00. Extreme height 78 inches, Top 30x20 inches, Height of case 53 inches, Mirror 20x18 inches. Shipping weight 225 pounds.

H57 Dressing Table Chair

Come-Packt Price $6.50. Dealer's price $11.00 Height of seat 18 inches, extreme height 30 inches Seat 16½x15½ inches. Shipping weight 25 pounds. Not shipped in sections.

Other colors of enamel can be furnished—French Gray, Robin Egg Blue, Cream White, but these colors are furnished to order and not kept in stock. Allow at least three to four weeks for these finishes as a good finish cannot be applied in less time. Other articles in this catalog can be finished in Enamel at an additional cost,—write for prices.

H635 Dresser

Come-Packt Price $35.50. Retail value $55.00. Extreme height 68 inches, Top 40x22 inches, Height of case 35 inches, Mirror 28x22 inches. Shipping weight 190 pounds.

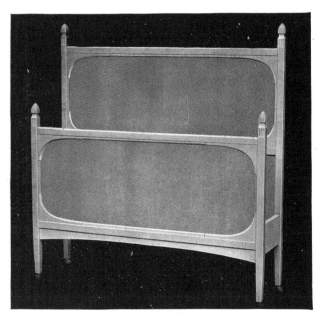

Bed H634

Come-Packt Price $24.75. Full size 4 feet 6 inches. Retail price $40.00, Height of head 51 inches, Foot 39½ inches. Shipping weight 160 pounds. All beds accommodate a 6 foot 2 inch mattress. Single bed (3 feet 6 inches, $23.25. Shipping weight 140 pounds.) These beds not furnished with cane panels. Write for special price on other beds or pieces finished in white enamel.

New Come-Packt Designs

Those who have been privileged to see the pieces shown on this and the following pages as they left our designing and pattern rooms have praised the generous proportions, the easy and graceful curves, the careful workmanship and above all, the substantial worth and old fashioned "comfy" feeling of these splendid rockers and chairs.

Not everyone admires the pure Mission, or Arts and Crafts lines, and it was to give everyone an opportunity to take advantage of our Manufacturers' wholesale prices that we brought out these pieces and we have tried to make them just a little bit better than ordinary and we know that your appreciation of these designs will increase as time goes on.

Every piece in this catalog is accurately described as to materials used and the quality of the materials. If a piece is plain sawn oak, we say frankly that it is plain oak. Quarter sawn where quartered oak is used. Veneering, or laminated pieces are plainly designated so that in each case you may know exactly what you are paying for.

These chairs are shipped completely assembled and ready for use. They cannot, on account of their spring seat construction, be shipped in any other manner. You have a choice of our regular finishes in the oak chairs, but the solid mahogany is finished and rubbed, unless a bright finish is especially requested. Any oak piece in this catalog will be filled, varnished and hand rubbed at 10 per cent net extra to our lowest regular price. Please bear in mind that it takes from 14 to 17 days for the varnish finish and only the mahogany, birch mahogany and white enamel pieces are kept in stock completely finished.

H4701

Come-Packt Price $15.75. Cowhide Covers, $20.35. D. B. Leather $18.45. Roan Skin $18.50. Height 34 inches. Width 37 inches. Shipping weight 85 pounds. Specify kind and color of cushions and finish when ordering. Assembled only. Quartered white oak.

H4703

Come-Packt Price $15.75. Imperial leather cushions. Cowhide covers $20.35. D. B. Leather $18.45. Roan skin $18.50. Height 34 inches. Width 37 inches. Shipping weight 85 pounds. Shipped assembled only. Mention kind and color of cushions and finish when ordering. Quartered white oak.

H4702

Come-Packt Price $16.25. Imperial leather cushions. Dealer's price $26.50. Cowhide covers $20.50. D. B. Leather $18.50. Roan Skin $18.75. Height 34 inches. Width 37 inches. Shipping weight 85 pounds. When ordering, specify kind and color of cushions and finish. Assembled only. Quartered white oak

H4801

Come-Packt Price $17.90. Figured or striped denim. Dealer's price $30.00. Imperial leather $19.70. Roan skin $29.75. Panne Plush $31.60. This superb Colonial design is furnished in *Solid Mahogany,* only, with loose pillow cushion over springs. Beautifully finished in a deep lustrous satiny hand-rubbed Mahogany that brings out all the exquisite richness of this splendid cabinet wood. Height 38 inches. Width 36 inches. Shipping weight 85 pounds. Not shipped in sections.

H4802 Come-Packt Price (Same as Rocker above) Chair to match Rocker H4801.

H4704

Come-Packt Price $15.95. Imperial leather cushions. Dealer's price $26.25. Cowhide covers $20.25. D. B. Leather $18.50. Roan skin $18.50. Height 34 inches. Width 37 inches. Shipping weight 85 pounds. Delays will be avoided if you will mention color and kind of cushions and finish. These chairs are shipped assembled only. Quartered white oak.

H4803

Come-Packt Price $21.75. Figured or striped green denim. Dealer's price $45.00. Imperial leather $22.90. Roan skin $29.75. Panne Plush $32.50. These fireside chairs and rockers are reproductions of two famous designs in the Kensington Museums, London, England—they are of solid Mahogany and Nos. 4803 and 4804 are beautifully hand carved. Modern designers have failed to excel the old masters who first produced these splendid examples of art in furniture. Height 39 inches. Width 26 inches. Shipping weight 85 pounds. Oak or solid Mahogany.

H4804

Come-Packt Price $21.65. Same as H4803 Rocker. Imperial leather $22.90. Roan skin $29.75. Panne Plush $32.50. Admirers of rare old Mahogany will see in these pieces more than the art of the workman who fashioned the carvings so skillfully,—they are heirlooms of a substantial sturdy construction that will never be supplanted by the genius of the modern school of designing. Shipping weight 85 pounds.

H4805

Come-Packt Price $22.25. Figured or striped green denim. Dealer's price $45.00. Imperial leather $23.40. Roan skin $30.25. Panne Plush $33.00. This rocker and the chair No. 4806 similar in design and construction to the two piece preceding except that the straight arms have been supplanted by gracefully curved rests and no carvings relieve the severity of the splendidly turned posts. Shipping weight 85 pounds. Oak or solid Mahogany.

H4806—Come-Packt Price (Same as rocker above). Chairs to match rocker H4805.

H4705

Come-Packt Price $16.85. Imperial leather cushions. Dealer's price $27.75. Cowhide covers $21.35. D. B. leather $19.50. Roan skin $19.50. Height 41 inches. Width 38 inches. Shipping weight 90 pounds. Specify kind and color of cushions and stains when ordering. Quarter sawn white oak only.

H4706

Come-Packt Price $17.25. Imperial leather cushions. Dealer's price $27.75. Cowhide covers $21.75. D. B. leather $19.85. Roan skin $19.85. Shipping weight 90 pounds. Height 41 inches. Width 38 inches. Specify kind and color of cushions and finish when ordering. Quarter sawn white oak. Not shipped in sections.

H4707

Come-Packt Price $16.65. Imperial leather cushions. Dealer's price $27.50. Cowhide covers $21.10. D. B. Leather $19.25. Roan skin $19.35. This chair is not shipped in sections. Please specify the kind and color of cushions and finish when ordering. Height 41 inches. Width 38 inches. Shipping weight 90 pounds. Quartered white oak.

H4708

Come-Packt Price $17.15. Imperial leather cushions. Dealer's price $27.75. Cowhide covers $21.65. D. B. Leather $19.80. Roan skin $19.95. Height 41 inches. Width 38 inches. Shipping weight 90 pounds. Not shipped in sections. Please mention the kind and color of cushions and finish when ordering. Quartered white oak.

H4709

Come-Packt Price $16.70. Imperial leather cushions. Dealer's price $27.50. Cowhide covers $21.15. D. B. Leather $19.30. Roan skin $19.40. Height 41 inches. Width 38 inches. Shipping weight 90 pounds. Please mention kind of cushions and finish when ordering. This rocker is quarter sawn white oak and cannot be shipped in sections.

H4710

Come-Packt Price $17.05. Imperial leather cushions. Dealer's price $27.75. Cowhide covers $21.55. D. B. Leather $19.70. Roan skin $19.85. Height 41 inches. Width 38 inches. Shipping weight 90 pounds. Specify kind and color of cushions and finish. Quarter sawn white oak. Shipped assembled only.

H4711

Come-Packt Price $16.95. Imperial leather cushions. Dealer's price $27.75. Cowhide covers $21.45. D. B. Leather $19.60. Roan skin $19.75. Height 41 inches. Width 38 inches. Shipping weight 90 pounds. Quarter sawn white oak. Please mention the kind and color of cushions and finish.

H4713 Sleepy Hollow Rocker

Come-Packt Price $17.25. Figured or striped denim. Dealer's price $38.00. Roan skin $23.75. Panne Mohair Plush $24.60. Height 38 inches. Width 36 inches. Shipping weight 90 pounds. Not shipped in sections. Your choice of plain oak or mahoganized birch. Seat is upholstered over springs and nicely tufted with moss and curled hair. This design is rightly called a "Sleepy Hollow Chair."

H4712

Come-Packt Price $16.75. Imperial leather cushions. Dealer's price $27.50. Cowhide covers $21.25. D. B. Leather $19.40. Roan skin $19.50. Height 41 inches. Width 38 inches. Shipping weight 90 pounds. Quartered white oak. Specify the kind and color of cushions and stains when ordering.

H4810 and H4811

Come-Packt Price, Solid Mahogany, $13.25 each. Figured or striped denim covers. Dealer's price $32.50. Imperial leather covers $14.25. Cowhide $17.45. Roan skin $14.50. Panne Mohair Plush $16.00. Chair and rocker are same price and same dimensions. Height 36 inches. Width 23½ inches. Shipping weight 65 pounds. These dainty patterns with soft rounding arms and claw feet, are splendid examples of the better class of mahogany furniture. The seats are upholstered in the best manner over highly tempered springs. The workmanship and finish have been followed out with characteristic Come-Packt sincerity.

H4812

Come-Packt Price, Solid Mahogany, $17.75. Figured or striped denim covers. Dealer's price $55.00. Imperial leather covers $19.95. Cowhide $24.50. Roan skin $26.50. Panne Mohair Plush $24.50. Width 47 inches. Shipping weight 85 pounds. This is a beautiful type of a settee with graceful, easy lines that is worthy of the period that produced the Master artist whose influence has been indelibly impressed in Modern designing of fine furniture.

H4807 and H4808

Come-Packt Price, Solid Mahogany, $17.50 each. With figured or striped denim. Dealer's price $35.00. Imperial leather $18.50. Cowhide $21.75. Roan skin $19.75. Panne Mohair Plush $20.50. Measurements and shipping weights same as the suit above. We take considerable pride in offering this splendid Chippendale suit to our friends and we believe that the skill, taste, and effort made to bring out this artistically shaped suit will be appreciated. The cabriole legs and beautifully hand carved balusters, the graceful outward sweeping arms and well balanced proportions makes this suit a treasure for the most critically furnished home.

H4809

Come-Packt Price, Solid Mahogany, $24.75. Striped or figured denim. Dealer's price $55.00. Imperial leather $26.10. Cowhide $32.75. Roan skin $28.90. Panne Mohair Plush $29.90. This suit is made up with loose spring seat cushions and every effort has been made to bring out all the effectiveness of the design by finishing the wood in the most workmanlike manner. Please mention the color and kind of cushions when ordering. On all mahogany pieces a choice is offered of a dull rubbed or bright finish, but the dull finish will invariably be sent unless otherwise specified.

H4814 and H4813

This old Virginia Colonial pattern in solid Mahogany is a beautiful reproduction of some of the earlier patterns of the Colonies. It shows in every line the care, skill and patience of the workman in shaping the splendidly curved arms and backs to conform to the outlines of the person using them. The graceful lines and beautifully shaped posts and claw feet add to the attractiveness of these wholesome designs. The cushions are upholstered over highly tempered steel coil springs. The work is done entirely by hand and the completed work is of the highest quality and perfection.

H4815

	Denim	Imperial Leather	No. 1 Cowhide	Roan Skin	Panne Mohair Plush
H4813 Rocker	$18.60	$19.25	$25.50	$22.75	$24.25
H4814 Chair	18.60	19.25	25.50	22.75	24.25
H4815 Settee	27.50	28.25	38.90	34.50	36.25

Height 35 inches; width (chairs), 27 inches; (settee), 45 inches. Shipping weight (chairs) 65 pounds; (settee), 85 pounds.

Spring Seat Oak Rockers

These massive designs have found especial favor where a large, roomy and comfortable rocker is desired. The seats are upholstered over highly tempered steel coils that give an invitation to rest as soon as you sink into their generous depths. It is impossible, of course to furnish chairs of this or similar design in solid quarter sawn oak, so the exposed parts are faced with beautifully figured quartered white oak. These chairs are made complete in our Toledo factory where all of the details of construction and finish receive careful supervision. Your choice of our regular finishes at the prices quoted; or a beautiful hand rubbed varnish finish will be furnished on any oak design in the catalog at 10 per cent extra. All goods are kept in the white and when a rubbed varnish finish is ordered, please allow not less than 12 to 15 days as a good rubbed finish cannot be applied in less time. These chairs cannot be shipped in sections.

H4601

Come-Packt Price $16.15. Imperial leather. Dealer's price $24.50. Cowhide covers $21.55. D. B. Leather $19.60. Roan skin $19.75. Height 40 inches. Width 28 inches. Seat 21x23 inches. Shipping weight 90 pounds. The front posts are of solid quartered oak and the hand carved claw feet give a touch of ornamentation that is not out of place with this style of a rocker. Specify covering and finish when ordering.

H4602

Come-Packt Price $15.00. (Imperial leather). Dealer's price $23.50. Cowhide covers $20.35. D. B. Leather $16.95. Roan skin $16.95. Height 40 inches. Width 24 inches. Seat 20x20 inches. Shipping weight 90 pounds. This splendid rocker is slightly lighter in construction than the others shown on this page, but it is a massive design and well suited for the largest rooms. Our best spring seat construction is used on these chairs and the workmanship and finish is unsurpassed. Not shipped in sections.

H4603

Come-Packt Price $17.75. (Imperial leather.) Dealer's price $26.50. Cowhide covers $23.50. D. B. Leather $21.00. Roan skin $21.00. Height 40 inches. Width 28 inches. Legs 2⅝ inches. Shipping weight 105 pounds. This rocker cannot be shipped in sections. Please mention finish and cushion materials when ordering.

H4604

Come-Packt Price $16.15. (Imperial leather). Dealer's price $25.50. Cowhide covers $22.25. D. B. Leather $19.60. Roan skin $19.60. Height 39 inches. Width 28 inches. Legs 2¾ inches. Shipping weight 105 pounds. This piece and the No. 4603 are shown with tufted and buttoned back cushion, but the plain backs will be furnished when especially ordered at the same price. We can give the dimensions, but cannot describe the solid comfort of these splendid rockers.

H4605

Come-Packt Price $16.75. (Imperial leather). Dealer's price $26.00. Cowhide covers $22.75. D. B. Leather $19.75. Roan skin $19.75. Height 42 inches. Width 28 inches. Shipping weight 100 pounds. Not shipped in sections. Be careful to mention the kind and color of cushions and stains when ordering. It takes from four to six days to apply a satisfactory mission finish after your order has been received.

H4608

Come-Packt Price $19.75. (Imperial leather). Dealer's price $32.00. Cowhide covers $26.35. Panne Plush $25.95. Height 38 inches. Width 48 inches. Shipping weight 100 pounds. Solid oak with quartered faces or mahoganized birch. Mention the kind and color of cushions and finish when ordering. Panne mohair plush furnished in dark red or green only, finest quality silk fabric

H4606

Come-Packt Price $13.90. (Imperial leather). Dealer's price $24.50. Cowhide covers $17.95. Panne Plush $17.60. Shipping weight 85 pounds. This suite is a regular stock design and one piece may be ordered at a time, if desired. We can always match up colors and cushions at a later date. Oak or Mahoganized Birch.

H4607

Come-Packt Price $13.45. (Imperial leather). Dealer's price $24.00. Cowhide covers $17.50. Panne Plush $17.15. Shipping weight 85 pounds. Height 38 inches. Width 26 inches. The graceful contour of the arms and posts, and the hand carved claw feet give this suit a very attractive appearance and it is needless to say that the construction and finish are up to the COME-PACKT Standard. Oak or Mahoganized Birch.

H5101 Mission Couch

This is one of our latest designs in a Mission couch, and meets with the popular demand for a couch for office, den or library use. It is easily kept clean on account of not being tufted. It is built for wear and will give splendid service. Not shipped in sections.

The seat and head rest are splendidly upholstered over long steel springs, with a full spring edge. The springs are hand tied and covered with moss and cotton felt.

A reasonable store price for this design would be $48.00. Remember in comparing prices that quality should be the first consideration. *Come-Packt Price $25.90.* Imperial leather. Cowhide $46.90. D. B. Leather $39.25. Shipping weight 145 pounds. Length 77 inches. Width 30 inches.

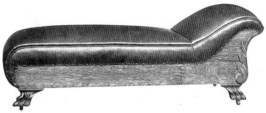

H5103 Couch

This is a good substantially built couch in laminated quartered oak that is designed to give good service with a little more than the ordinary usage that falls to the lot of a couch in an office or den.

The cushions are upholstered over highly tempered hour glass springs, and with a full spring edge, they should not sag down or get out of shape. Length 77 inches. Width 30 inches. Shipping weight 145 pounds. Ordinary Retail price $42.50.
Come-Packt Price $23.60. Imperial leather. Cowhide, $44.65. D. B. Leather $36.90. These couches are not upholstered in the Roan skin.

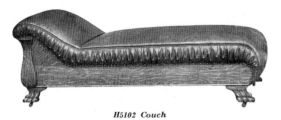

H5102 Couch

The hand carved claw feet, the deeply ruffled seat border and the shaped pilaster are not true to the Mission lines, but some prefer more ornamentation than is permissible with Mission styles and this design is bound to be deservedly popular.

Both sides are alike and are veneered over hard wood. This couch cannot be shipped in sections. The upholstering is up to the COME-PACKT standard and that means that it is the best. Retail price $55.00.
Come-Packt Price $25.50. Imperial leather. Cowhide $50.45. D. B. Leather $41.25. Shipping weight 145 pounds. Length 77 inches. Width 30 inches.

4613   4612

4614

Three Piece Suit in Birch Mahogany only. A medium priced suit of good proportions with a gracefully curving top rail and a Mahogany Veneer baluster that adds to the attractiveness of these three pieces. The settee is 42½ inches wide and 37 inches high. The seats are loose cushions upholstered over highly tempered steel springs. These pieces cannot be shipped in sections. Shipping weight, settee 95 pounds; chair 75 pounds. The usual price for a similar suit would be $67.50.

	Imperial Leather	Cowhide	Panne Plush	Denim
Settee No. H4614	$12.90	$18.10	$15.70	$12.00
Chair No. H4612	8.50	11.25	10.35	8.00
Rocker No. H4613	8.95	11.75	10.75	8.40

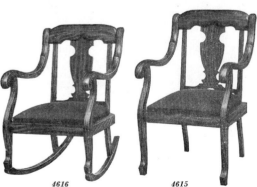

4616   4615

4617

Three Piece Suit in Birch Mahogany only. A substantially built suit, similar to the suit above, except for the top rail and back panels. (Back panels Mahogany veneer). These suits are handsomely finished in the best varnish and you have a choice of a bright or hand rubbed dull finish. The seats are of the most durable steel spring construction. Settee width is 42½ inches. Height 37 inches.

Shipping weight, Settee 95 pounds. Chair or Rocker 75 pounds. Dealer's price for suit $67.50.

	Imperial Leather	Cowhide	Panne Plush	Denim
Settee No. H4617	$12.95	$18.25	$15.85	$12.10
Chair No. H4616	8.55	11.35	10.45	8.10
Rocker No. H4615	9.10	11.85	10.85	8.50

H4620

An artistically designed three piece suit in Birch Mahogany only. With gracefully moulded scroll arms and claw feet. The back balusters are veneered with genuine mahogany.

Unless a bright finish is ordered, we invariably ship the dull rubbed finish. The loose cushions are upholstered over all steel spring construction and are serviceable, comfortable and attractive

H4618 and H4619

in appearance. Height 37 inches. Settee 42½ inches wide. Shipping weight 95 pounds. Chair or rocker 85 pounds.

	Denim	Imp. Lea.	Cowhide	Roan	Panne Plush
H4618 Rocker	$11.85	$12.25	$15.25	$14.25	$13.85
H4619 Chair	11.35	11.75	14.75	13.75	13.25
H4620 Settee	17.35	17.85	23.35	21.75	21.35

H4611

Come-Packt Price $22.75. Figured or striped denim. Dealer's price $35.00. Imperial leather $23.50. Cowhide $30.75. Roan skin $28.50. Panne Mohair Plush $27.75. Width 49½ inches. Shipping weight 115 pounds. This suit is handsome mahogany finish and as the grain of the birch very closely resembles that of genuine mahogany, the finished appearance is almost identical with that of the solid mahogany. Either dull rubbed or bright finish. Please mention finish and kind and color of cushions when ordering.

H4609 and H4610

Come-Packt Price $15.95 each. Denim covers. Dealer's price $22.50. Imperial leather $16.50 each. Cowhide $20.25. Roan skin $21.25. Panne Mohair Plush $20.50 each. Height 37 inches. Width 27 inches. Seat 21½x21½ inches. Shipping weight 85 pounds. These finely moulded scroll arm Colonial chairs and settees are made of solid mahoganized birch. They are massive and substantial and make an ideal parlor suit. The usual spring seat construction is used, making a comfortable, roomy chair or rocker for everyday purposes.

H4623

A handsome Birch Mahogany three piece parlor suit that will be a pleasing addition to any living room or parlor. The workmanship and finish show unmistakably the care with which all COME-PACKT Furniture is built.

We wish to be remembered by our work and every detail is carried out with a thoroughness that assures permanent satisfaction. We believe in work well done and we believe that your appreciation

H4621 and H4622

of our work will grow as you become familiar with the standard of excellence that the Come-Packt Trade Mark typifies.

Height 36 inches. Width 24 inches. (Settee), 45 inches Shipping weight (chairs), 75 pounds; (settee), 90 pounds.

	Denim	Imp. Lea.	Cowhide	Roan	Panne Plush
H4621 Rocker	$13.95	$14.55	$24.60	$19.50	$18.25
H4622 Chair	13.45	14.00	24.10	18.95	17.75
H4623 Settee	20.25	20.75	32.00	29.50	28.45

Over-Stuffed Rockers

The illustrations on this page, and the one following, give but an imperfect idea of the beauties and real worth of these splendidly built rockers. As in all COME-PACKT PRODUCTS, time nor money have been spared to give each piece that indefinable quality that makes it more desirable, more exclusive, and more stylish than you can buy elsewhere at the same low price. It is our desire to make it easier for you to buy from this catalog, than to patronize the Middleman. A year's trial of all furniture and your money back any time you say,— this liberal offer has no strings attached and it is made by a responsible House,—one that you will find it a pleasure to do business with.

These Rockers are made in the D. B. Leather only—Red, Brown, Green or Black in the smooth grain. See color page 73 for description of color materials.

H4501 Colonial Over-Stuffed Fireside Rocker

Come-Packt Price $22.30. D. B. Cowhide only. Dealer's price **$45.00.** Height 40 inches. Width 34 inches. Shipping weight 85 pounds. A remarkably good value for the price. The best long oil tempered steel springs are used in the seat cushion and over them is laid moss and cotton felt. The seat is so constructed that it should give a life time of service without sagging down and becoming unsightly. An appropriate chair for the library or den. **Birch Mahogany** Rockers.

H4502 German Comfort Rocker

Come-Packt Price $22.50. D. B. Cowhide only. Dealer's price **$45.00.** Height 36 inches. Width 32 inches. Shipping weight 90 pounds. A splendidly made, comfortable rocker that may be used in the same room with Mission designs and blends or harmonizes remarkably well with them. The seat is softly padded over long coil springs, insuring the maximum of comfort and restfulness. The style of upholstering is German or Deutsche Kunst.

H4503 Over-Stuffed Tub Rocker

Come-Packt Price $26.50. D. B. Cow hide only. Dealer's price **$48.00.** Height 34 inches. Width 34 inches. Shipping weight 80 pounds. This "Tub" rocker is a late design that is rapidly becoming very popular for den, library or smoking room,—the back is low, but for a reading or lounging chair, it would be difficult to design a more comfortable or restful rocker. The back and sides are neatly tufted and the chair as a whole is especially harmonious in its proportions and pleasing lines.

H4504 Bachelor Club Rocker

Come-Packt Price $22.25. D. B. Cowhide only. Dealer's price **$45.00.** Height 36 inches. Width 32 inches. Shipping weight 80 pounds. The easily rounding back of this design and the projecting wings make an artistic as well as a luxuriously easy rocker that invites relaxation. It is a well balanced, handsome chair that will give the service you should reasonably expect of a high grade article of furniture.

"These Goods are Advertised."

Clean advertising—advertising as straight and true as the word from mother to son—must soon be the only advertising to which men may justly apply the name. *"These goods are advertised"* must carry a meaning equivalent to the sterling mark on silver. The leaders in advertising thought and merchandising efficiency are agreed that nothing less can be permitted.

A spark was struck centuries ago from which the torch of clean advertising has been lighted. "Thy neighbor as thyself" is the heart, —the glowing, lambent fire whose warmth makes the blood of commerce flow with invigorating strength through the body of civilization. *"Who trades fairly may trade freely."*

No truer words than these spoken by the Dallas, Texas, Advertising League could characterize the Merchandising policy of the Come-Packt Furniture Company.

H4505 Den Rocker

Come-Packt Price $23.75. D. B. leather only. Dealer's price $47.50. Height 41 inches. Width 32 inches. Shipping weight 100 pounds. The loose pillow over an auxiliary spring seat gives added resiliency and comfort. This design is intended more for den and club use than for ordinary living room, chiefly on accoun of the massive construction. Your choice of red, brown, green or black, D. B. leather only on any design on this or the preceding page. Not shipped in sections.

H4506 Turkish Rocker

Come-Packt Price $29.75. D. B. Leather only. Dealer's price $55.00. Height 41 inches. Width 32 inches. Shipping weight 100 pounds. This is one of the famous Harrington Spring rockers which is so constructed that the chair frame will rock in any direction. The entire front and the edge of the back are deeply ruffled and the back is softly tufted with a head roll rising slightly above the height of the wings. A substantial, roomy, well balanced chair that is almost as comfortable as a bed.

H4507 Turkish Rocker

Come-Packt Price $23.25. D. B. leather only. Dealer's price $47.50. Height 41 inches. Width 32 inches. Shipping weight 95 pounds. A Harrington Spring Rocker with finely tufted back cushion and deep ruffled border with fringed apron. This is a splendid value and well worth considerable more than the Come-Packt Price. In Comparing Prices, compare the quality so that you may be sure which article is the best value for the price asked.

H4508 English Overstuffed Fireside Rocker

Come-Packt Price $18.50. D. B. leather only. Dealer's price $34.50. Height 40 inches. Width 32 inches. Shipping weight 95 pounds. This is one of our best library rocker designs and one that is bound to be popular wherever this style of a chair is appropriate. The heavy spring seat and finely upholstered arms and back are severely plain in their treatment, but the effect is pleasing to the eye and the proportions are correct in every detail. The COME-PACKT GUARANTEE is behind every article we list and the purchase price and freight charges will be immediately refunded if any purchase is unsatisfactory.

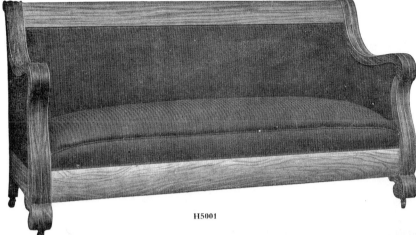

H5001

Come-Packt Davenports

This line of artistically designed colonial davenports on this and the following page shows the diversified talent and skill of our designer. The handsome and graceful lines and proportions have not been spoiled by the bungling hand of unskilled craftsmen. From the time the rough lumber leaves our kilns until the' wood is fashioned into its ever varying forms and then passes into the skilled hands of our finishers, every process is watched with minute care to see that the finished product shall be worthy of the Come-Packt Trade-Mark.

H5001 Plymouth

Come-Packt Price $45.75. (Plain Oak or Mahoganized Birch with figured denim covers). Dealer's price $90.00 Imperial leather covers $47.60. Cowhide covers $62.00. Panne Plush $59.30. D. B. Leather $53.60. These large pieces cannot be furnished with Roan skin covers. Height 32 inches. Width 78 inches. Depth 30 inches. Shipping weight 285 pounds. Your choice of Dull or Bright finish.

H5002 Virginia

Come-Packt Price $49.00. (Genuine Solid Mahogany only). Denim covers. Dealer's price $110.00. Imperial leather covers $53.25. Cowhide covers $68.85. D. B. Leather $61.40. Panne Plush $65.95. (Not furnished in Roan skin.)

This unusually attractive davenport is made of the finest solid mahogany and beautifully finished with either a dull hand-rubbed, or bright finish. The seat and side cushions are cleverly upholstered over the best coil springs that insure a life time of service and comfort. These designs require the highest type of skill, and we believe you will appreciate the splendid workmanship, materials and finish when you have one of these choice designs in your home. The dull-rubbed finish will invariably be furnished in the genuine mahogany unless other finishes are particularly specified in your order. Height 32 inches. Width 78 inches. Shipping weight 285 pounds.

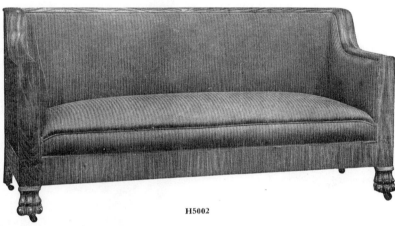

H5002

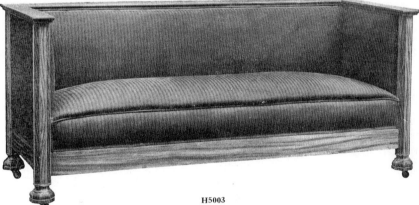

H5003

H5003 Royalton

Come-Packt Price $45.70. (Solid oak or genuine Mahogany with denim covers). Dealer's price $95.00. Imperial leather $49.75. Cowhide $62.75. D. B. Leather $57.50. Panne Plush $62.30. (Roan skin covers not furnished). Height 32 inches. Width 78 inches. Shipping weight 285 pounds.

An unsurpassed Colonial design that shows in every line the structurally perfect product of skilled workmen. The one great object of our organization is to build furniture that shall stand pre-eminent among the better classes of house furnishings,—furniture the artistic qualities of which are an inspiration and the influence of which will extend into the lives of future generations. The prices of these pieces are lower than the sterling quality of the workmanship materials and finish would seem to warrant. The genuine Mahogany will be shipped unless your order clearly specifies OAK and the kind of cushions and finish desired.

H5004 Puritan

Come-Packt Price $45.75. (Solid Oak, or genuine solid Mahogany with denim cushions). Dealer's price $95.00. Imperial leather covers $49.90. Cowhide covers $63.00. D. B. Leather $57.60. Panne Mohair Plush $62.50. Height 32 inches. Width 78 inches. Depth 30 inches. Shipping weight 285 pounds.

The davenports on this and the following page are not shipped in sections. The sturdy "livable" qualities of this unusually charming design appeal at once to the love of home and home-like things. The severely plain lines are enhanced by the fine proportions and skillful handling of the cabinet work and finish. The cushions are soft and inviting and the variety of covering materials and finishes assures a selection that will harmonize with the color scheme of your home. Please mention the material, finish and kind and color of cushions when ordering.

See color sheet at the end of catalog for description of coverings and finishes.

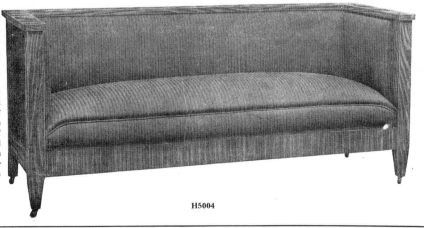

H5004

Fine Furniture
Exclusive Designs
Factory Prices

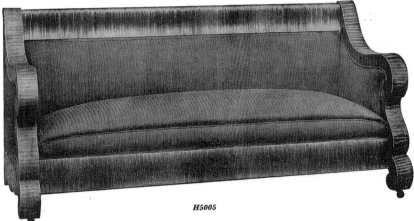

H5005

H5005 Newport

Come-Packt Price $58.80. (Quartered Oak or Genuine Mahogany with denim covers). Dealer's price $125.00. Imperial leather $63.45. Cowhide $77.45. D. B. Leather $70.60. Panne Plush $74.80. (Roan skin not furnished.) Height 32 inches. Width 78 inches. Depth 30 inches. Shipping weight 285 pounds. An artistic specimen of the cabinet-makers' art,—the beautiful Oak and Mahogany veneers have been cleverly fashioned around the rests and front columns which produces a result not obtainable in the solid materials. The deep toned color of the Mahogany is enhanced by the subtle art of the finisher and the beautiful hand-rubbed effect lends a tone of exclusiveness and dignity to any home, but with all its luxurious ease, the design has not paused at mere physical comfortableness.

H5006 Dartmouth

Come-Packt Price $60.35. (Quartered Oak or Genuine Mahogany with denim covers). Dealer's price $130.00. Imperial leather covers $64.60. Cowhide $80.15. D. B. Leather $72.75. Panne Mohair Plush $77.30. (Roan skin not furnished). Height 32 inches. Width 78 inches. Depth 30 inches. Shipping weight 285 pounds. These davenports cannot be shipped in sections. It is to be regretted that we must review our achievements in designing through the eye of the Camera and it is doubly regrettable that so much furniture that is unworthy in its artistic merit is marketed under false colors by unscrupulous manufacturers and merchants. Good furniture is not necessarily expensive but some makers skimp their designs, slight details and misrepresent the grade or quality of their products. Whether our prices seem high or low, it has been our desire to give full measure of value for every dollar of our prices and to describe all articles accurately so that the buyer may know the real quality of his purchase. The Come-Packt guarantee is sufficient evidence of quality and fair dealing for everybody.

H5006

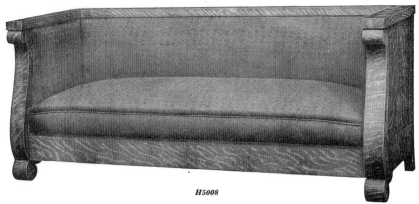

H5007

H5007 Mt. Vernon

Come-Packt Price $78.45. Crotch Mahogany (only), with denim covers. Dealer's price $150.00. Imperial leather $79.90. Cowhide $94.50. D. B. Leather $88.50. Panne Mohair Plush $89.90. (Not furnished in Roan skin.) Height 32 in. Width 82 in. Depth 30 inches. Shipping weight 295 pounds. This davenport cannot be shipped in sections. Come-Packt Furniture is a quest for those qualities that are most desirable in goods of the better class,—no appeal is made to cheapness as a quality and our low prices are made possible only by our methods of sale and delivery. This massive and beautifully finished design shows unmistakably the superb skill of our craftsmen. The mechanical difficulties that strew the paths of those who attempt to use crotch mahogany are little appreciated by the average furniture buyer. A perfect specimen is almost a triumph of mind over matter.

H5008 Hampton

Come-Packt Price $50.60. Quartered Oak or Genuine Mahogany with denim covers. Dealer's price $105.00. Imperial leather $52.30. Cowhide $68.20. D. B. Leather $61.70. Panne Mohair Plush $62.95. Not furnished in Roan skin. Height 32 inches. Width 78 inches. Depth 30 inches. Shipping weight 275 pounds. Not shipped in sections. The pleasing nicety of detail, the color and finish, the harmony of outline and proportion combine to make this davenport a desirable one for the formal occasion as well as for the ordinary uses of the every-day living room. The cushions are upholstered over highly tempered steel springs and no detail of the cabinetmakers or upholsterers' art has been neglected that would make this a better or more desirable piece of furniture. Please specify, when ordering, the kind of wood, finish and color and kind of finish. The davenports on this and the preceding page are all finished in the best dull, hand-rubbed varnish, unless other finishes are specially required.

H5008

Our New Willow Furniture

The following pages are devoted to a few superb *Willo-Weave* designs and for excellence of materials and workmanship, symmetry and beauty of outline, these pieces are in a class with our justly famous Mission and Bungalow furniture, and discriminating taste could not select two types of furniture, so radically different in materials and construction, that would harmonize more perfectly in the same rooms.

These pieces are all made of selected imported French stock and are entirely hand made by workmen who learned the art of weaving it in their native land. Nowhere else except in the genuine willow can you find the style, durability, quality and that indefinable something that makes it so different from the reed, fibre or rattan furniture.

Willo-Weave is not intended as an appeal to cheapness—the cost of the imported stock and the whole hand-work process makes it impossible for these pieces to compete in price with the machine made reed, fibre or rattan furniture.

Finish—Willo-Weave will be finished in your choice of the following colors: Dark Chocolate Brown (harmonizes with our dark weathered) Light Chocolate Brown (harmonizes with our Nut Brown, Flemish and Fumed Oak) Forest Green (harmonizes with Early English and Green Weathered) Tan (harmonizes with Golden Oak) Mahogany and Silver Gray. Specify plainly the color desired or willow furniture will be shipped unstained. The willow is finished in a dull gloss varnish that gives a rich satiny appearance to the wood.

Cushions—Each piece (except where specified otherwise), is listed without a cushion. Many will prefer to make their own cushions or pads out of some of the light colored and dainty patterns in Chintz, Chambray, Cretonne, or in the figured or plain denims

or tapestry fabrics. However, at the extra prices specified below, we will furnish cushions to fit the different pieces: Figured denim, $1.00 each; Imperial leather, $1.25; genuine cowhide, $2.25, and genuine imported roan skin, $2.00. Cow and roan cushions in piece pattern 15% less than above prices.

Prices—For the price shown under each piece we will completely finish the furniture in any color specified above, or we will ship the piece "in the white." Many will prefer the piece unfinished in the natural color of the willow itself and where the willow is to be used in a room with white or cream enameled furniture; the natural color would be preferable. Cushions furnished at the extra prices shown below. Samples of the figured denims will be sent on request.

All prices are f.o.b. Ann Arbor, Mich., or Toledo, O., and include packing. All willow pieces will be shipped completely "set-up" and will take a higher freight rate than the sectional Mission furniture, but as the willow pieces are so extremely light, the total freight on a single piece will hardly equal the freight on a similar piece in oak. The weights shown are the shipping weights and include weight of cushion.

Specify the color of stain desired or all WILLO-WEAVE will be shipped in the white, unstained.

Cushions for any of the chairs, unless otherwise specified, will be furnished at following prices:

Figured Denim	$1.00
Imperial Leather	1.25
Cow Hide	2.25
Roan Skin	2.00

All "Willo-Weave" Furniture is shipped UNSTAINED unless otherwise ordered.

We make swing seats to match any chair at $2.50 extra to list price, including hooks, chains and all necessary fittings.

W5201

Come-Packt Price $9.75. (Without cushion.) Rocker 75 cents extra. Dealer's price $16.50. Height 36 inches, Seat 20x19 inches. Shipping weight 30 pounds

W5203

Come-Packt Price $13.75. (Without cushion.) Dealer's price $19.50. Rocker 75 cents extra. Height 36 inches, Seat 20x19 inches. Shipping weight 30 pounds.

W5204 Reading Chair

Come-Packt Price $10.85. (Without cushion.) Dealer's price $17.75. Rocker 75 cents extra. Seat 20x18 inches. Shipping weight 25 pounds.

W5205

Come-Packt Price $8.75. (Without cushion.) Dealer's price $14.75. Rocker 75 cents extra. Height 35 inches. Seat 20x19 inches. Shipping weight 25 pounds.

W5206 Basinette

Come-Packt Price $10.85. Dealer's price $17.75. Height 27 inches. Basket 12 inches deep. Top 37x17 inches. Shipping weight 25 pounds.

W5207

Come-Packt Price $11.75. (Without cushion.) Rocker 75 cents extra. Dealer's price $18.50. Shipping weight 25 pounds.

These Willo-Weave patterns are among the most popular designs that we have ever listed. They are light, dainty and comfortable and will outwear any rattan, fiber or reed furniture.

We make up cushions in white cloth at 75 cents each and the real covering may be put on by the purchaser. This is done as an accommodation to our customers who may wish to make use of their own covering materials.

W5208
Come-Packt Price $11.25. (Without cushion.)
Dealer's price $18.25. Shipping weight 30 pounds.

W5209 Fireside Chair
Come-Packt Price $14.50. (Without cushion.)
Dealer's price $22.50. Height 40 inches. Seat 21 x 21 inches. This chair has wide arms and two pockets at either side. Shipping weight 35 pounds.
Specify the color of stain desired, when ordering, or all Willo-Weave will be shipped unstained.
Cushion for any of the chairs, except where otherwise specified, will be furnished at the following prices:

Figured denim _____ *$1.00*
Imperial leather _____ *1.25*
Cow hide _____ *2.25*
Roan skin _____ *2.00*

W5210 Sleepy Hollow Chair
Come-Packt Price $12.85. (Without cushion.)
Dealer's price $20.75. Shipping weight 35 pounds.

W5211
Come-Packt Price $10.25. (Without cushion.)
Dealer's p ice $17.00. Rocker 75 cents extra. Shipping weight 30 pounds.

W5212 Window Seat
Come-Packt Price $8.75. Dealer's price $14.75 Height 24 inches, Seat 26 x 18 inches. Shipping weight 25 pounds.

W5213
Come-Packt Price $10.50. (Without cushion.)
Rocker 75 cents extra. Dea er's price $17.25 Shipping weight 25 pounds.

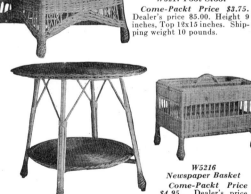

W5217 Foot Stool
Come-Packt Price $3.75.
Dealer's price $5.00. Height 9 inches, Top 12x15 inches. Shipping weight 10 pounds.

W5216 Newspaper Basket
Come-Packt Price $4.95. Dealer's price $7.75. Height 14 inches, Top 13½x20 inches.

W5214 Fireside Chair
Come-Packt Price $11.25. (Without cushion.)
Rocker 75 cents extra. Shipping weight 30 pounds.

W5215
Come-Packt Price $8.25. 27-inch top. 30-inch top, $8.50. 33-inch top, $9.00 36-inch top, $10.00. Dealer's price $14.25. Height 27 inches, small size, 28 and 29 inches for largest top.

W5218 Sewing Rocker
Come-Packt Price $7.90. (Without cushion.) Dealer's price $14.25. Height 33 inches, Seat 18x17 inches. Straight chair to match $7.15. Shipping weight 20 pounds.

Bungalow and Mission Lighting Fixtures

No one thing adds or detracts more from the general effect of an otherwise perfectly harmonious room than the lighting fixtures. Rooms that would otherwise be perfect in appointments are frequently marred by the conventional and incongruous combination polished brass electrolier and chandelier.

It was to meet this condition and to provide suitable fixtures to match our *Come-Packt Furniture* that we show here a splendid line of portable lamps, domes, showers, and other special designs that may fit into an otherwise incomplete corner or wall space.

Materials—White oak is the material used in making these fixtures and the same careful skill and attention to detail is followed out in their construction as distinguishes our other lines of furniture and fittings. We have endeavored to show a comprehensive line that would be suitable for most any room or occasion.

Equipment—All fixtures, whether electric, gas or oil are complete and ready for installation (except that we do not furnish electric bulbs unless specially mentioned under the description of the fixtures.) Such parts as electric sockets, wiring, plugs, etc., gas hose, goose neck, mantel, burner, chimney and oil fount, burner, wick and chimney, etc., are furnished with the different types of fixtures without extra charge. Insulating joints are included with combination fixtures.

Measurements—The length of a fixture means the distance between extreme points. If measuring for domes, send distance from end of gas pipe to floor, or from ceiling to floor. All domes, unless otherwise ordered, are furnished for nine foot ceilings.

Extra length of wood chain furnished at 45 cents per foot. Our prices are for the fixtures finished in your choice of stains: Dark Weathered, Fumed, Early English, Nut Brown, Flemish, Green Weathered or Golden. Ruby art glass or combination of Ruby, 20 per cent extra. Rochester burners for oil fixtures, $1.00 extra.

If desired, the fixtures will be shipped in the white and may be finished up with your other furnishings to match the interior wood work of your home.

Finish—ALWAYS MENTION FINISH, COLOR OF GLASS (a choice of green, amber, or green and brown, unless otherwise mentioned in the description of the fixtures) and color of beads. *Dark weathered finish will be sent* on your order and we will use our own judgment as to color of glass, etc., *unless your order is specific in this regard.* Always order by catalog number.

Shipping—These fixtures are securely packed for shipment and very seldom are damaged in transit, however, if breakage should occur, either refuse to accept the shipment, or require the Freight Agent to write a full description of the damage on your freight bill. We do not hold ourselves responsible for goods damaged in transit, but will make good any damage at our expense when freight bill is returned to us with notation as to damage by your Agent.

Shipments amounting to less than $10.00 will not be sent C. O. D. or on payment of 25 per cent of purchase price unless collection charges are assumed by the purchaser.

H4903 Portable

Come-Packt Price $14.50. (Art glass.) With 4-inch Seed Beads, $1.35 extra. 4-inch Cut Beads, $4.50 extra. Dealer's price $20.00. Height 26 inches, Shade 18 inches, Base 7¼x7¼ inches, diameter of standard 2 inches. Two electric or one light gas. This portable has pull sockets. Shipping weight 30 pounds. Mention kind of fixture when ordering.

H4926 One Light Gas or Electric Bracket

Come-Packt Price $4.75. (Plain art glass.) Leaded art glass, $6.25. Extends 9 inches, from wall. Shade 6x6x6. Wall plate, 6x6 inches. Shipping weight 15 pounds. Mention whether for electricity or gas.

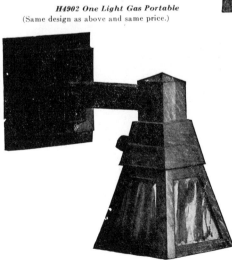

H4901 Two Light Electric

Come-Packt Price $6.65. (Leaded art glass.) 4-inch Seed Beads $1.00 extra. Amber or green glass only. Height 23 inches, Shade 16 inches, Base 7½ inches. Shipping weight 25 pounds.

H4902 One Light Gas Portable

(Same design as above and same price.)

H4905 Gas or Electric Portable

Come-Packt Price $3.85. (Art glass.) Dealer's price $6.50. Height 22 inches, Shade 14½x14½ inches, Base 7x7 inches, Stem 1¾x1¾ inches. One light electric, gas or oil. Green, amber, or green and brown art glass furnished only. Shipping weight 25 pounds. Mention kind of fixture when ordering.

H4904 Electric Wall Bracket

Come-Packt Price $3.75. (Art glass.) Dealer's price $6.75. One light electric, extends 9 inches from wall, Shade 5x5x5 inches. Shipping weight 25 pounds.

H4906 Two Light Electric Portable

Come-Packt Price $6.65. (Plain art glass and 4-inch Seed Beads.) Height 22 inches, Spread 18 inches, Base 7 inches. Shipping weight 20 pounds. A splendid lamp for a large library table.

Specify in your order the color of stain and glass desired, or dark weathered stain and green glass will be furnished.

Small articles like the Foot Rests and Lamps should be ordered with other pieces, as the freight charges will be very small compared with freight when shipped alone.

H4908 Two Light Electric

Come-Packt Price $6.75. (Plain art glass without beads.) Leaded art glass (without beads) $8.35, Seed beads $1.00 extra. Height 29 inches, Shade 18½x18½ inches. Shipping weight 25 pounds.

H4907 Portable

Come-Packt Price $5.50. (Art glass.) Dealer's price $8.00. Height 21 inches, Shade 11x11 inches, Stem 3½x3½ inches, Base 7x7 inches. One light, electric, gas or oil. Green, amber, or green and brown art glass furnished only. Shipping weight 25 pounds. Rochester round wick burners $1.00 extra.

Always mention whether fixture is for gas, electricity or oil.

H4909 Portable

Come-Packt Price $9.00. (Leaded art glass, 4-inch Seed Fringe.) With ruby art glass and 4-inch Seed Fringe $12.50. Dealer's price $15.00. Height 24 inches, Shade 21 inches diameter,—7 inches deep, Base 8x8 inches. Two light electric or one light gas. Green art glass only at above price. Shipping weight 35 pounds.

H4910 Two Light Electric

Come-Packt price $4.00. (Plain art glass.) With leaded art glass and apron as shown, $5.35. (Green art glass and ruby diamond center.) Height 24 inches, Shade 14x14 inches, Base 7x7 inches. Shipping weight 25 pounds.

H4911 Dome

Come-Packt Price $4.75. (Dealer's price $6.50.) Length 48 inches, Dome 14x14 inches, Depth 8 inches. One light electric, plain art glass with bead fringe. Shipping weight 45 pounds. Arranged for 9 foot ceiling.

H491 2 Pendant

Come-Packt Price $3.95. (Art glass.) Dealer's price $6.75. One light electric. Length 18 inches, Ceiling plate 4½x4½ inches, Shade 6x6x6 inches. Shipping weight 20 pounds.

H4913 Portable

Come-Packt Price $2.80. (Plain art glass, no fringe.) 3-inch Seed Beads $1.00 extra. Dealer's price $5.50. Height 19 inches, Shade 12x12 inches, Base 6x6 inches. One light, electric or gas only. Mention kind when ordering. Green, amber, or green and brown art glass furnished only. Shipping weight 25 pounds.

Specify color of glass, kind of fringe and color of stain, or dark Weathered finish and our choice of glass will be sent.

H4914 Two Light Electric

Come-Packt Price $5.00. (Plain art glass.) Height 25 inches, Shade 16x16 inches, Base 7x7 inches. Shipping weight 20 pounds.

Extra length of wood chains 45 cents per foot. 4 inch seed bead fringe 35 cents per lineal foot.

H4915

Come-Packt Price $4.25. (Art glass.) 3-inch Seed Beads $1.00 extra. Dealer's price $6.25. Height 24 inches, Shade 14x14 inches, Base 7x7 inches. One light, electric or gas. Green, amber or green and brown art glass furnished only. Shipping weight 25 pounds.

H4916 Two Light Electric

Come-Packt Price $8.35. (Plain art glass without beads.) Beads $1.00 extra. Height 23 inches, Shade 18 inches, Base 8x8 inches. Shipping weight 25 pounds.

Single hangers with chain and ceiling plate like corner drops of H4917 Shower (shown below) $3.75 each.

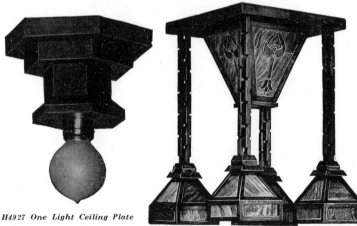

H4927 One Light Ceiling Plate

Come-Packt Price $2.75. (Globe not included.) Ceiling plate 5½ inches. Drop of socket 4½ inches. Shipping weight 10 pounds.

H4917 Shower

Come-Packt Price $18.75. (Plain art glass.) Leaded art glass as shown, $4.25 extra. Dealer's price $35.00. Length 24 inches. Ceiling plate 18x18 inches, Lantern 11x11x10 inches, Small shades 7x7 inches. Five light electric ceiling Shower. Shipping weight 60 pounds.

H4918 Pendant

Come-Packt Price $6.50. (Plain art glass.) (Leaded art glass, $1.50 extra.) Dealer's price $9.50. Length 24 inches. Lantern 5x5x16 inches. One light electric. Shipping weight 25 pounds.

H4919 One Light Desk or Piano Lamp

Come-Packt Price $6.50. (Plain art glass.) Length extended 24 inches, Shade 7x10x6 inches. Slide 10 inches. Shipping weight 20 pounds.

H4920 Pendant

Come-Packt Price $7.50. (Leaded art glass.) With plain art glass, $6.00. Dealer's price $12.00. Lantern 7½x7½x8 inches, Length 18 inches. One light electric. Shipping weight 25 pounds.

H4921 Portable

Come-Packt Price $3.50. (Art glass.) 3 inch Seed Beads $1.00 extra. Dealer's price $6.00. Height 22 inches, Shade 14½x14½ inches, Base 7x7 inches, Stem 1¾x1¾ inches. One light electric, gas or oil, mention kind when ordering. Green, amber, or green and brown art glass furnished only. Shipping weight 25 pounds.

H4922 Portable

Come-Packt Price $4.75. (Art glass.) Dealer's price $6.50. Height 24 inches, Shade 15x15 inches, Depth of apron 2½ inches, Base 7x7 inches. One light, electric, gas or oil, mention kind when ordering. We furnish only green, amber, or green and brown art glass with this portable. Shipping weight 25 pounds.

H4923 Electric Dome

Come-Packt Price $10.85. (Leaded art glass without beads.) Seed Beads $1.25 extra. Length 60 inches, Depth 10 inches, Diameter 18 inches, Ceiling plate 7 inches. One or four lights as ordered.

This same dome 23 inches in diameter, other dimensions the same as above. Come-Packt price $13.50 (without beads.) Seed beads $2.00 extra. If wanted in ruby glass 20% extra. One or Four lights as ordered.

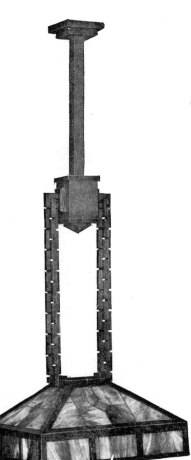

H4924 Gas Dome

Come-Packt Price $8.50. (Plain art glass.) (As oil dome, $2.00 extra.) Dealer's price $14.50. Length 54 inches, Spread 20x20 inches, Apron depth 4 inches. Made only in green leaded art glass. Shipping weight 60 pounds. (Not furnished for electricity. See H4925

H4928 Four Light Ceiling Plate

Come-Packt Price $6.65. (Bulbs not included.) Size of plate 12 in. Drop to bottom of socket 4½ in. Shipping weight 20 pounds.

NOTE: All domes are arranged for 9 foot ceilings. Extra wood chain 45 cents per foot.

H4925 Dome

Come-Packt Price $8.50. (Leaded art glass.) Dealer's price $14.50. Length 54 inches, Spread 20x20 inches, Aprons 4 inches. Two light electric. Shipping weight 50 pounds.

Cluny Lace Curtains

In presenting the following illustrations of our Cluny Lace Curtains, we feel that we are filling in an adequate way a long standing demand on the part of our customers for something of real intrinsic worth in this line of hand made goods, but at prices that would be low for machine made imitation of them.

Beauty of design, excellence of workmanship and range of patterns to say nothing of our low prices, characterize the entire line and places before you a splendid selection of curtains. The discriminating purchaser will here find the height of satisfaction in hand wrought fabrics, real Cluny laces, combining, as they do, old traditions of the French Peasantry with modern ideas of superb design.

There is no secret as to why we can sell our curtains at the extremely low prices listed under the description of each curtain—there are no middlemen's profits. Our laces come direct to our mill, where they are made into curtains to be delivered direct to our customers—there are not five or six profits to be added to the selling price before the curtains reach your windows. The curtains are produced by workmen lifelong in the business and the COME-PACKT guarantee stands behind every pair.

All laces listed as *real Cluny* are absolutely hand made and pure linen, and are mounted on the best quality French nets made especially for us, or where specified the mountings may be of the best quality of etamine.

The cotton laces are mounted on a light net but the values are exceptionally good.

Dimensions—The dimensions given in the description of each curtain are the measurements of the single curtain—thus the dimensions of 2½ yards by 45 inches, means that each curtain of the pair is 2½ yards long and 45 inches wide.

Prices—All prices are quoted by the pair and the price is the same for the white, ecru or Arabian (tan). Be sure and state the color wanted when ordering or white net will invariably be sent to you.

Shipping—Express rates are practically the same as mailing rates but where two or more pairs are ordered, it is usually best to ship via express, delivery is safer and we *advise* this means of shipment. Mail or express charges for any curtain will be 25 cents per pair in addition to list price.

Samples—There is practically no waste in the cutting of our laces, and on account of their cost we cannot send samples indiscriminately of the laces; however, all curtains are sold subject to approval of the purchaser and may be returned at our expense if not satisfactory. All orders amounting to less than $10.00 must be accompanied by cash in full or collection charges must be assumed by the purchaser.

GC 100

Come-Packt Price $1.25 per pair. Dealer's price $2.25. 2½ yards by 36 inches. White or ecru. Has 1½-inch hems and cotton lace same width.

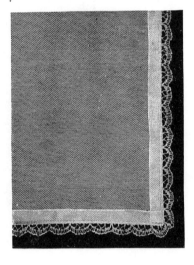

GL 202

Come-Packt Price $2.15 per pair. Dealer's price $3.25. 2½ yards by 45 inches. Furnished in white or ecru. Hand made Cluny lace one inch wide.

GL 200

Come-Packt Price $2.50 per pair. 2½ yards by 45 inches. French net.

GG 104

Come-Packt Price $1.25 per pair. Cotton furnished in white or ecru. (Same pattern as above.)

GL 210

Come-Packt Price $3.15 per pair. Dealer's price $4.50. 2½ yards by 45 inches. White or ecru. Has 3-inch hems and six petal lace, hand made.

GL 212

Come-Packt Price $3.50 per pair. Dealer's price $5.35. 2½ yards by 40 inches. White or ecru. Standard French net. A smart curtain.

GL 214

Come-Packt Price $3.60 per pair. Dealer's price $5.45. 2½ yards by 45 inches. Standard net in white or ecru. Real lace 2 inches wide.

GL 404

Come-Packt Price $3.65 per pair. Dealer's price $5.50. 2½ yards by 45 inches. White or ecru. Heavy French net and real linen laces 1½ inches wide.

GF 522

Come-Packt Price $7.75 per pair. Dealer's price $14.00. 2½ yards by 37 inches. White or ecru. Beautiful pure Cluny laces. One of the best curtains shown.

GS 506

Come-Packt Price $3.90 per pair. Dealer's price $7.35. 2½ yards by 38 inches. White or ecru. Finest etamine with 2-inch hem and 2-inch real Cluny lace.

GL 226

Come-Packt Price $6.85 per pair. Dealer's price $10.35. 2½ yards by 45 inches. White or ecru. Mounted on heavy French net with 2-inch hems.

GF 605

Come-Packt Price $2.25 per pair. Dealer's price $4.00. 2¾ yards by 44 inches wide. A heavy CABLE NET design of rare beauty and serviceability. Comes in white or Arabian.

GF 609

Come-Packt Price $2.40 per pair. Dealer's price $4.50. 3 yards by 52 inches wide. A combination of style, quality and finish in this splendid NOTTINGHAM curtain. White.

GF 611

Come-Packt Price $3.80 per pair. Dealer's price $5.75. 3 yards by 50 inches wide. An exceptionally sheer NOTTINGHAM with an effective Lily design on a delicate mesh net. White and two tone.

GF 602

Come-Packt Price $5.85 per pair. Dealer's price $8.25. 3 yards by 50 inches wide. A beautiful IRISH POINT curtain with floral motif applique on fine French net. White only.

GF 601

Come-Packt Price $4.80 per pair. Dealer's price $7.50. 2½ yards by 44 inches wide. An IRISH POINT of conventional leaf and trellis motif applique on fine French net. Ivory only.

Come-Packt Sewing Machines

Give long service and lasting satisfaction. They are of high quality and are fully warranted for ten years. Every machine carefully crated and prompt shipment guaranteed.

In offering our customers a selection of "Come-Packt" sewing machines, we have been at great pains to satisfy ourselves that they are not only as good as, but better than any other sewing machines, in order that they should be as pleasing and satisfactory to our customers as our line of "Come-Packt" goods has always been.

These sewing machines are reasonably priced, in fact are cheaper, quality considered, than it is possible to purchase other machines. Every conceivable labor saving device known to the sewing machine world is incorporated in their manufacture. We know that we can absolutely recommend them, and for this reason do not hesitate to warrant every machine absolutely, as shown by fac-simile copy of our warranty appearing on the following page.

"Come-Packt" sewing machines are exceedingly simple in construction, and all troublesome features of sewing machines of former years have been eliminated so that they never get out of adjustment or cause trouble of any kind to the operator. They stitch perfectly, fast and quietly, and on account of their careful construction, are exceedingly easy running. We feel that we cannot too strongly recommend them from the cheapest machine to the best one.

No. H4202 Come-Packt Model "B", Price $17.85

The "Come-Packt" model "B" machine is without question the best machine offered at anywhere near our selling price.

The sewing head of this machine is what is styled an extra high arm, and is carefully finished with the best of black enamel, relieved by brilliant ornamentation and high quality varnish. Among many other labor saving devices we wish to call attention to the automatic bobbin winder, special gear releasing device, special tension regulator, self setting needles and large self-threading cylinder shuttle, as well as the automatic stitch regulator. This sewing head will perform any class of family sewing.

The woodwork used on this machine is a five drawer, drop head pattern, strongly made and handsomely designed, and is equipped with a special automatic lifting device by means of which the sewing head is raised to sewing position at the same time that the lid of the machine is opened. This furniture is made of carefully selected oak with a quarter sawn lid and is carefully finished in a polished golden oak shade with the best of varnish.

The stand of the machine is strong and very substantial with high quality, brilliant black japan. The large belt wheel is swung on two sets of hardened steel ball-bearings which makes the machine exceedingly easy running.

Each one of these machines is furnished with a complete set of accessories and attachments with which an operator can do any class of fancy sewing possible on a sewing machine, and in addition each machine is positively warranted for TEN YEARS. We recommend this model to any one wishing an especially good machine at a very reasonable price.

Shipping weight, 120 lbs.

No. H4201 Come-Packt Model "A", Price $15.65

The "Come-Packt" model "A" sewing machine illustrated above, is the cheapest machine we offer, but regardless of this fact, is backed by the same warranty accompanying every other "Come-Packt" machine. It may be possible so to manufacture cheaper sewing machines than this one by eliminating a great many parts and being less careful as to the mechanical correctness of details. Such sewing machines, however, are made only to sell, but we have no hesitancy in stating that this one is made to sew. This machine is a five drawer, drop head machine with a carefully built case of selected oak, finished in a polished golden color with fine varnish. An 18-inch tape measure is placed on the front of the table under the varnish for the convenience of the operator.

The stand is strong and heavy and consequently very substantial, and is covered with a fine quality of brilliant japan.

The sewing head is carefully constructed and is equipped with a convenient tension and take-up, short self-setting needles, automatic bobbin winder and self-threading shuttle.

Each machine is equipped with a complete set of accessories and attachments absolutely free of charge.

Shipping weight, 100 lbs.

"Come-Packt" model "C" machine shown is a new design, which cannot help on account of the especial beauty of style and finish, but prove an exceedingly popular one.

The set of furniture used on this machine is quite different than the preceding models shown, and is one that is immediately pleasing to every prospective purchaser. It has four large, strongly constructed side drawers, and a handsome ornamental drop apron front which makes a symmetrical and pleasing appearance when the machine is closed. When the machine is opened the action of raising the lid automatically brings the sewing head into position ready for work, and at the same time lifts the drop apron front underneath the head, giving the operator ample knee room. This set of furniture is constructed of selected white oak, finished in a polished golden color with the best class of varnish, and the lid as well as the ornamental apron front drawer front are all quartersawn. For the convenient use of the operator an 18-inch tape measure is placed under the varnish on the front of the table.

The sewing head used for this machine is an extra high arm head which is exactly the same as is used on "Come-Packt,"

model "B". It has many modern labor saving devices including the automatic stitch regulator, automatic bobbin winder, simple tension, short, self-setting needles, large self-threading cylinder shuttle, and special gear releasing device for use in winding bobbin. The sewing head is especially strong in construction, every bearing surface is hardened and the head is nicely decorated in black enamel and bright colors with a finish of brilliant varnish baked on. It is a dependable, satisfactory sewing machine.

The stand is graceful in design and especially strong and well constructed. The large belt wheel is hung on two sets of ball-bearings which make it especially easy running, and the dress guard is so made that it fully protects the wheel, and at the same time prevents the belt from coming off, thus doing away with any necessity of the operator belting the stand wheel.

With each machine we furnish entirely free, a complete set of accessories and all attachments consisting of a filled oil can, illustrated instruction book, 2 screw drivers, 6 bobbins, 12 needles, cloth guide, quilter, ruffler, binder, tucker, braider, shirring slide and four hemmers of different widths.

The price on this machine is exceedingly reasonable for a machine of this quality and every purchaser will be entirely pleased.

Shipping weight, 120 lbs.

No. H4203 Four Drawer Automatic Lift, Come-Packt Model "C", Price $19.50

The "COME-PACKT" WARRANTY
Which Accompanies Every "Come-Packt" Sewing Machine

Certificate of Warranty

We hereby Warrant this fine Family Sewing Machine, number.........., to endure the wear and tear of family use for TEN YEARS from the date of purchase, and agree to replace, FREE OF CHARGE during that time, any defective parts, excepting only the wear and breakage of Needles and Shuttles.
Toledo, Ohio.   COME-PACKT FURNITURE CO.

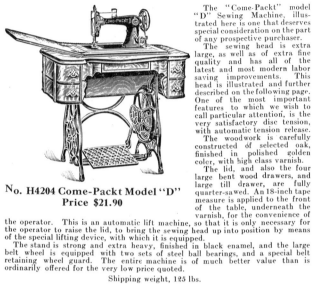

No. H4204 Come-Packt Model "D"
Price $21.90

The "Come-Packt" model "D" Sewing Machine, illustrated here is one that deserves special consideration on the part of any prospective purchaser.

The sewing head is extra large, as well as of extra fine quality and has all of the latest and most modern labor saving improvements. This head is illustrated and further described on the following page. One of the most important features to which we wish to call particular attention, is the very satisfactory disc tension, with automatic tension release.

The woodwork is carefully constructed of selected oak, finished in polished golden color, with high class varnish.

The lid, and also the four large bent wood drawers, and large till drawer, are fully quarter-sawed. An 18-inch tape measure is applied to the front of the table, underneath the varnish, for the convenience of the operator. This is an automatic lift machine, so that it is only necessary for the operator to raise the lid, to bring the sewing head up into position by means of the special lifting device, with which it is equipped.

The stand is strong and extra heavy, finished in black enamel, and the large belt wheel is equipped with two sets of steel ball bearings, and a special belt retaining wheel guard. The entire machine is of much better value than is ordinarily offered for the very low price quoted.

Shipping weight, 125 lbs.

No. H4205 Come-Packt Model "E"
Price $23.80

"Come-Packt" model "E" Machine, is, we fully believe, the lowest priced machine offered, quality considered, that is equipped with a full quarter-sawn set of furniture. This set of furniture is of exceedingly high grade construction, being carefully finished in golden oak and hand polished. It has four large side drawers, and also a small swing center drawer, and is equipped with our special tape measure, applied to the front of the table.

The design is plain, but of such a nature that it appeals to the most discriminating purchaser.

The stand of this machine is also ball-bearing, very heavy in construction and handsomely finished in black Japan. It runs easily and quietly.

The sewing head, which is illustrated on the following page, is not only as well made, but in reality, is of better construction than those used on many machines selling for very much higher prices. It will do every class of family sewing perfectly, and is absolutely guaranteed against defects of any kind.

The finish is very handsome, being all black enamel, relieved by colored decorations and covered with transparent varnish.

With this machine, as with every other machine illustrated, we furnish entirely free of charge, a complete set of the highest grade, all steel nickel plated attachments, with which an operator can do any class of fancy sewing possible on a sewing machine.   Shipping weight, 121 lbs.

The "Come-Packt" model "F" machine is not only a high grade machine, but is equipped with an especially high grade and attractive set of furniture. This particular design is not only novel, but matches up with the very best of furniture and therefore fits perfectly in the home.

This set of furniture is built throughout of selected quarter-sawn oak, carefully finished in a golden shade and hand polished; only the very best of materials and varnish are used. It has four large bent wood side drawers, as shown, which conform to the circle or crescent pattern of the table ends These drawers are very substantial and their design is such that they add great beauty to the machine. The ornamental drop apron front, which in the illustration, is shown, is in reality lifted up automatically underneath the sewing head, when the machine is opened. This is accomplished through the use of our special automatic lifting device, so that it is only necessary for the operator to raise the head of the machine, to bring the sewing head up into position, as well as to lift the drop front up out of the way. An 18-inch tape measure is applied to the front of the table and will be found to be a great convenience.

The "Come-Packt" head, illustrated on the following page, is distinctively a high grade sewing machine. It has an extra high arm, is particularly well finished with black enamel, with colored decorations and fine varnish, and in addition, all bright metal parts are handsomely nickel plated.

Among many other features, which will be found useful, we call particular attention to the automatic bobbin winder, automatic stitch - regulator, positive cam-driven take-up, disc tension with automatic tension release, capped needle and presser bars, large self-threading cylinder shuttle, self-setting needle, steel forged positive four-motion feed, and a special device for throwing machine out of gear when winding bobbins. Every bearing surface of this machine is carefully hardened and fitted.

The stand is extra heavy, nicely finished in brilliant black Japan, baked on. The large stand wheel is hung on two sets of steel bicycle ball-bearings, enclosed in patented ball retainers, which insure easy running, as well as quietness and the pitman or driving rod connecting the treadle and belt wheel, is a self-aligning non-breakable steel type. The dress guard covers the wheel thoroughly, protecting the operator's skirts, and is so constructed that it prevents the belt from coming off of the wheel, therefore doing away with the necessity of re-belting machine whenever used. We furnish free, a complete set of accessories and attachments, consisting of filled Oil Can, illustrated Instruction Book, 2 Screw Drivers, 6 Bobbins, 12 Needles, Cloth Guide, Quilter, Ruffler, Tucker, Binder, Braider, Shirring Slide and 4 Hemmers of different widths. This machine is guaranteed to do any class of family sewing and with these attachments, can be done any class of fancy sewing, possible on a machine.

Shipping weight, 120 lbs.

No. H4206 Four Drawer Automatic Lift Come-Packt Model "F" Price $24.65

Kitchen Cabinets

Every woman who does her own housework should have the necessary utensils for her work conveniently at hand. No argument can be made against the convenience of a modern Kitchen Cabinet. Order a cabinet to come along with the rest of your order and save the unnecessary work and drudgery of the kitchen. The Cabinets shown on this page are excellent values and will give you the best of satisfaction. The top sections and bases are shipped in compact crates and take the lowest possible freight rate.

Heidelberg Blue Ware Kitchen Set; (26 pieces) as shown with No. H4003 cabinet, furnished with any cabinet on this page, extra per set _____$3.25

(One set only sold with each cabinet.)

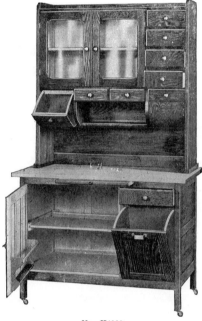

No. H4003

Oak Front. Finished in Golden Oak Waxed. Interior of top and inside of doors varnished. This Cabinet is equipped with the popular Swinging Flour Bin, which may be lowered for convenience in filling. It also has a tilting sugar bin. Copper Hardware. Working space, 42 x 25. Height 70 inches. Shipping weight, 180 lb.

Price $17.25
Extra for Nicolene top on base 1.25
Extra for Enameling Interior of Top 1.25

No. H4002

Oak Front. Finish, Golden Oak, Waxed. Interior of Top and Inside of Doors Varnished. Copper Hardware. Working Space, 42 x 25 inches. Height, 70 inches. Shipping Weight, 190 pounds.

Price...$18.25
For Enameling Interior of Top 1.25
For Enameling Interior of Base 1.25
For Nicolene Top on Base 1.25

No. H4001

Oak Front and Ends. Finish, Golden Oak, Waxed.
Shipped with Full Extension Nicolene Top and Two Compartment, Portable, Metal Bread and Cake Box, ONLY. Interior of Top and Inside of Doors Varnished. Copper Hardware. Glass Tea, Coffee and Spice Jars, Sugar Scoop and Rolling Pin in Top. Full Glass Front in Flour Bin. Sliding Cutting Board, Sliding Shelf, Galvanized Sheet Metal Bottom, Pan Rack and Casters in Base. Working Space, 40 x 37. Height, 68 inches. Crated Weight, 208 pounds.

Price $24.00
For Enameling Interior of Top, (extra)........................ 1.25
For Enameling Interior of Base, (extra) 1.25

No. H4004

A Substantial Kitchen Table. Oak Front Finish, Golden Oak Waxed, with Metal Flour and Meal Bins, and 2 Drawers for Kitchen Utensils and Cutlery. Working Space, 42 x 26. Height, 28½ inches. Weight, 65 pounds. Copper Hardware. Whitewood Top, nicely sanded and smoothed. Shipping weight, 65 lbs.

Price $5.65
Extra for Nicolene Top on Base 1.25

Mattresses and Springs

Kapok Mattresses

A third of our life is spent in bed and why should we deliberately secure anything but the maximum of comfort for so great a portion of our existence? There is as much difference in the comfort of mattresses as there is in the shoes we wear.

KAPOK (Javanese Silk Floss) besides possessing all the resiliency of the best grade of hair mattress is absolutely sanitary; it will not absorb moisture (it is four times as buoyant as cork and is used extensively in the marine cushions and mattresses which are on occasion used as life preservers); it is extremely light as compared with cotton or hair; it will not mat down nor become lumpy; the mattress can be easily handled or turned by one person; it is absolutely sanitary and, in a word, the KAPOK mattress has all the good features of any mattress and none of the bad ones. It is lighter, cleaner, more durable, more healthful and more comfortable than any mattress made.

Only the best grade of JAVA KAPOK is used and we guarantee the finished article to be more satisfactory than any mattress sold at any price. A strong statement, but the proof is in a trial. The mattress may be returned to us if we have misrepresented it in any way. The mattresses will weigh from 22 to 35 pounds depending upon the size.

H4377 Come-Packt Prices
100 per cent Kapok

3 feet wide, 5 inches thick_____$12.75
3 feet 6 inches wide, 5 inches thick_____ 13.50
4 feet wide, 5 inches thick_____ 14.50
4 feet 6 inches wide, 5 inches thick_____ 14.95
2 part mattresses extra_____25c.
Imperial roller edge extra_____25c

100% PURE COTTON FELT MATTRESSES

The laws of the State of OHIO require that all Mattresses made in the State shall be labeled before leaving the factory with a statement of the percentage of pure cotton or other materials used in the Mattress. This makes it impossible for a mattress made in the State of Ohio to be made or sold as a pure cotton felt mattress, unless it is PURE FELT, unless the manufacturer is willing to run the risk of fine and imprisonment.

The COTTON FELT MATTRESSES listed below are 100% pure cotton felt and they are as well made as it is possible to make a cotton mattress. They are built up of odorless, sanitary and elastic layers of pure cotton,—please note that these mattresses are "built" and not stuffed. This insures an even, soft and springy mattress that will not become hard and lumpy with continued use. Experienced mattress makers cover the layers of felt with a splendid quality of fancy ticking and after tufting to prevent a shifting of the layers of cotton it is ready for delivery to our customers. You can pay more for a genuine cotton mattress than our prices, but you cannot buy greater comfort and when the Dealer, or others charge more than our prices, they do so to make a greater profit. Why not keep this extra profit yourself? When you buy elsewhere be sure that you are getting cotton, or at least know what percentage is cotton and how much is excelsior or other substitutes.

H4378 Come-Packt Prices 100% Cotton. 4' 6" wide x 6' 2" (45 pounds), **$8.25.** 4' 0" wide x 6' 2" (45 pounds), **$8.25.** 3' 6" wide x 6' 2" (same basis), **$6.50.** 3' 0" wide x 6' 2" (same basis), **$4.50.** Imperial or roll edge mattresses 25 cents extra. Two part mattresses 25 cents extra.

H4354 Adjustable Steel Slats. Come-Packt Price $2.35.
Stronger and more sanitary than the old-fashioned wooden slats. They are made of heavily japanned No. 12 gauge steel 1¼ inches wide. Can be adjusted to fit any size bed from three to four feet and eight inches. Packed four slats to a set. Shipping weight 25 pounds.

H4354

Wirliger Spring Mattress
(PATENT APPLIED FOR)

H4375 Come-Packt Price $15.25 for 4 feet and 4 feet 6 inch size and $14.50 for 3 feet 6 inches and 3 foot sizes.

The center of this mattress is similar to our Jupiter spring, excepting that it contains 150 coils of very flexible highly tempered wire drawn specially for this purpose. This construction is incased in heavy muslin and covered entirely with a thick layer of grey curled hair, and this in turn is completely covered with a layer of best quality cotton felt. Full six-inch box with Imperial roll edge. Covered with highest quality fancy tick. This mattress will never pack or become lumpy. It is extremely comfortable and durable but inexpensive. Made in two pieces also, 50 cents extra. Shipping weight 90 pounds.

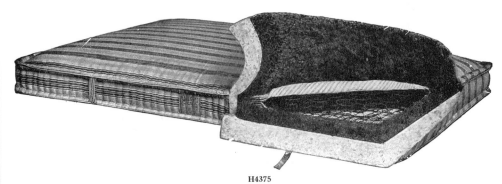

H4375

Ohio Box Spring

H4376

Come-Packt Price $12.50 for 4 ft. 6 inches and 4 ft. width; $12.25 for 3 ft. 6 inch width; $11.75 3 ft. size.

All Steel Sanitary construction, made on the same principle and of the same high quality material as the Hercules. The construction is covered with a ten pound layer of the best cotton felt and finished with Imperial edge in highest quality fancy ticking. Made in all regular sizes for metal and wood bedsteads. Shipping weight 100 pounds.

Mention kind of bedstead when ordering.

H4376

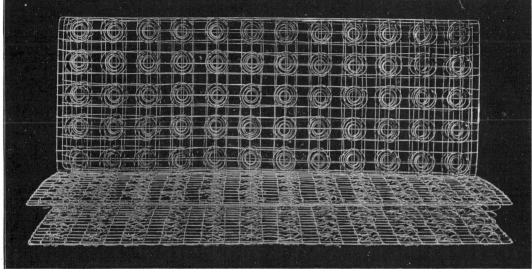

H 4351

H4351 Jupiter Spring
Come-Packt Price $3.65

For any of the following sizes: 3 feet, 3 feet 6 inches, 4 feet and 4 feet, 6 inches. Dealer's price $7.50. Shipping weight 60 pounds. These all steel springs are made of the best quality steel wire tempered by an improved process that gives a permanent elasticity to the coils and you need have no fear that the springs will sag after being in use a short time. This is the proper spring for use with a folding cot or lounge, as it is hinged in the middle. There are 120 coils of No. 11 gauge spring wire.

H4352 Vulcan Spring

Come-Packt Price $6.95. For any size as follows: 3 feet, 3 feet 6 inches, 4 feet, 4 feet 6 inches. Dealer's price $12.00. This is one of the most durable bed springs made. It has 90 coils of No.11 gauge steel wire, highly tempered in oil. The base or frame is made of steel angles and very strongly constructed. It has patent adjustable hanger straps and this spring may be used on either wood or metal beds without slats. The side angles and hangers are finished Vernis Martin. Shipping weight 70 pounds, 4 feet 6 inch size.

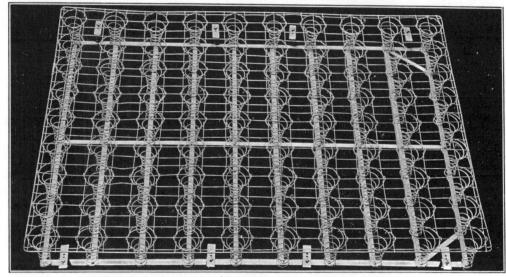

H 4352

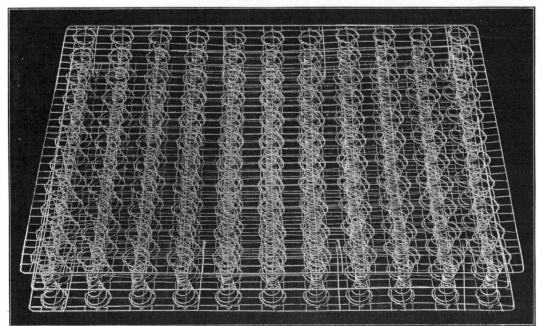

H 4353

H4353 Ajax Spring

Come-Packt Price $7.50.

For any size as follows: 3 feet, 3 feet 6 inches, 4 feet, 4 feet 6 inches. This spring was made especially for wooden beds, but a hanger frame similar to the one on the Vulcan Spring, in the illustration here can be furnished already applied to the spring for $1.00 in addition to list price. Each and every coil is knotted and connected together by an interlocking system of tie wires, which with special tempering results in a more comfortable and durable construction than can be obtained in any other way. The spring has 120 double coils 8 inches high. The centers are connected with special steel tie rods. Shipping weight, 4 feet 6 inch size, 70 pounds.

Ooze Skin

Ooze Skin Library Table Covers

The illustration at the left shows the general outline of Ooze leather table covers. They are brilliantly colored and a choice is offered of red, brown, green, black, gray or tan. The hides vary in size from 7 to 9 square feet, and they are soft and pliable as the finest suede leather.

COME-PACKT PRICE, any size_____$1.75 each.

PILLOW CUSHIONS

Stock pillow cushions for settees and davenports are 20x20 inches, and are reversible. (See illustration below at the left). Zig-Zag patch cushions, (See illustration below), will be furnished at the prices listed. They are made of die-cut pieces of genuine leather and are sewed on a special machine with a Zig-Zag stitch that brings the edges firmly together, and for all practical purposes these cushions are as strong and durable as the cushions made from the single piece of leather. They are artistic and many will prefer them for the novelty and attractive appearance of the Zig-Zag stitch.

Prices	Imperial Leather		Cowhide		Roan Skin	
Pillow Cushions	Plain	Zig-Zag	Plain	Zig-Zag	Plain	Zig Zag
18 x 18 inches	$2.40	Not Made	$4.75	$4.05	$3.90	$3.30
20 x 20 inches	2.75	"	5.50	4.65	4.75	4.05
22 x 22 inches	3.45	"	6.25	5.20	5.50	4.65

SPECIAL MADE TO ORDER CUSHIONS AND PADS

We will make pad cushions to order for special sizes at the following prices, when specific measurements are given or when paper patterns showing exact size and shape of irregular shaped cushions are furnished. *Purchase price in full must accompany all orders for special cushions.* All made-to-order cushions will be stuffed with thoroughly cleaned and sanitary cotton. Zig-Zag cushions 15% less than list prices, in genuine leather only.

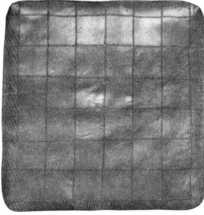

Spring cushions 20% in addition to prices shown below.

Box or round edge, as ordered,	Per Square Ft.
2-2½ inches thick Imperial leather, denim bottom	$.90
Same reversible	1.05
4 inches thick, Imperial leather, denim bottom	1.00
Same reversible	1.15
2-2½ inches thick, Cowhide, denim bottom	1.35
Same reversible	1.70
4 inches thick, Cowhide, denim bottom	1.50
Same reversible	1.85
2-2½ inches thick, Roan skin, denim bottom	1.25
Same reversible	1.50
4 inches thick, Roan skin, denim bottom	1.40
Same reversible	1.65
2-2½ inches Panne Plush, denim bottom	1.30
Same reversible	1.45
4 inches thick Panne Plush, denim bottom	1.40
Same reversible	1.75

In computing square feet, take extreme measurements of cushions to be ordered.

Plain Pillow Back Cushion   **Zig Zag Back Cushion**

COUCH HAMMOCK

It would be easy to make a cheaper couch hammock, but in the one shown below, we have combined quality of materials and workmanship into a completed article that is the equal of couches selling for double our price. A splendid grade of khaki duck is used throughout. The windshield is adjustable in height and one end has a convenient pocket for papers or small books. The pad is constructed in a workmanlike manner and is softly padded with 2 inches of cotton felt, and tufted with metallic buttons. We use a National Metal spring exclusively with folding metal legs fitted with casters. The legs may be lowered and the hammock used as a couch or cot. A special patented arrangement of springs prevent the edges from dragging down.

H4325 Couch Hammock

Come-Packt Price $10.50. Complete as shown above with adjustable windshield, ropes, and pad. Length 72 inches. Depth 30 inches. Shipping weight 60 pounds.

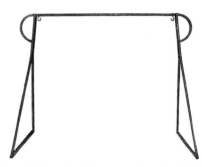

This metal standard is made of the best tubular steel, nicely finished in green lacquer. The truss construction makes it very rigid and durable. The stand is easily taken apart and may be moved from the veranda to the lawn, or packed away for the winter in a very small space. The standard is a convenience and not a necessity as the Couch may be hung from the porch ceiling or other convenient place.

H4326 Couch Standard

Come-Packt Price $3.85. Length 84 inches. Height 5 feet 6 inches. Spread of supports 4 feet 6 inches. Shipping weight 25 pounds.

Come-Packt Asbestos Table Covers and Mats

All housewives who use a GOOD ASBESTOS TABLE COVER will enjoy their meals far better if they know that there is a protection under the table cloth that will permit hot dishes to be placed at random on the table without injury to the top. For the convenience of our customers we carry the VERY BEST ASBESTOS TABLE COVER that is made.

This cover is composed of two layers of pure asbestos on each side of a layer of wool-felt, making a perfect insulation with a soft and durable surface. They are covered with heavy flannel jackets which may be removed and washed.

These covers lay perfectly smooth and flat; do not spoil the table setting in any way and can be folded to put away when not in use. All pads are put up in attractive boxes and prices quoted are for either round or square tops. Leaves furnished at the extra price quoted below.

PRICE LIST

44-inch diameter tops			$3.50 each
45 " " "			3.75 each
48 " " "			4.00 each
54 " " "			5.00 each
60 " " "			6.25 each
Leaves, 44x9			.80 each
Leaves, 45x9			.85 each
Leaves, 48x9			.90 each
Leaves, 54x9			1.00 each
Leaves, 60x9			1.10 each

For either round or square tables, give extreme diameter of tops when ordering and if leaves are wanted, state number and width of leaves. If tables have a beveled edge measure only to top of bevel.

Come-Packt Prepared Schellac—We cut our own schellacs in alcohol and blend the white and orange schellac in right proportions for use on stained woods. Mission finishes, particularly on furniture, should be schellaced before waxing.

Come-Packt Mission Furniture Polish—Mission furniture should never be washed with soap and water as the water will turn the schellac a milky color. Use a good grade of furniture wax two or three times a year, or use our specially prepared Mission Brightener and Polish.

Come-Packt Liquid Glue—is an adhesive that has no superior for furniture work. It is convenient to handle, inexpensive and invaluable to those who have frequent use for a high grade glue.

Price List of Stains, Finishes and Sundries

(The genuine ammonia process fumed oak is more or less difficult for an inexperienced person to apply, and we suggest that you write us for information before attempting to apply this color.)

Stains, any color listed (except fumed)	per ½ pint,	$0.25
(1 gallon should cover 700 square feet of hard wood;	" pint,	.40
400 feet soft wood.)	" quart,	.75
	" gal.	3.00

Liquid Wax, Mission-Lac, Prepared Schellac or Liquid Glue, same price for quantities as quoted above on stains.

Come-Packt Mission Polish	per pint,	$0.40
Prepared Furniture Wax (hard)	¼ pound,	.15
Stain Brushes	each,	.10
When ordering leather of any kind specify carefully the exact dimensions desired. Imperial leather (imitation), any color listed and in either the natural or "Spanish" grain, 50 inches wide; best quality,	per square foot,	.15
Gimp (Black, green, brown and red)	per yard,	.05
Metaline tacks (all colors)	per dozen,	.05
Roan skins, guaranteed, imported goat hides, any color listed "Pebbled" grain only,	per square foot	.45
Cowhides, any color listed, except black, and in either the "Smooth" or "Spanish" grain,	per square foot	.60
Figured or striped denim, red, green or brown, 36 inches wide	per yard,	.45
Panne Mohair Plush, steel blue, tan and dark red only, 28 inches wide	per yard	2.25

Extra Table Leaves—furnished at the following prices each: 44-inch, $.80; 45-inch $0.85; 48-inch $0.90; 54-inch, $1.00; 60-inch, $1.25 (plain sawn oak).

Unless otherwise specified, all orders for accessories, except stains, will be sent by mail when weighing less than four pounds. Postage rate 16 cents per pound. Stains cannot be sent by mail and will always be sent by express when ordered alone. Include enough money when ordering accessories to cover postage charge—we will promptly refund the difference, if you have enclosed too much.

Come-Packt Stains and Finishing Materials

The interior wood work and furniture, wherever possible, should be harmonious in color and finish. It is an easy matter to produce this effect when building a new home, and COME-PACKT SPIRIT STAINS will be found superior to any other stain or dye for finishing the wood work of your house. The stains are more penetrating than an oil stain, the colors are fast and beautifully rich and deep in tone. The stains may be applied by an inexperienced person and the resulting finish will be as handsome and durable as when used by the most experienced finisher.

Come-Packt Liquid Wax is the best and most durable wax for floors, furniture or interior wood work; it is water-proof and does not spot or turn white. It is applied with a soft cloth and forms a hard durable coating that is as soft and lustrous as an oil rubbed finish.

Come-Packt Wax is best when used over a first coat of schellac, but it may be used directly over the stains and gives the same effective finish, but it will spot more easily with water.

Come-Packt "Mission-Lac" is a high grade varnish coater that may be used directly over the stains, particularly where the furniture or wood work is to be exposed to the weather. It flows freely and does not show laps, drying free from dust in four hours and ready for use, or for waxing in 36 hours. No skill required in applying this coater.

Famous Ever-Grip Gliding Casters

Used on all Come-Packt chairs and tables, not provided with roll casters. They are noiseless, easy on floors and carpets, easily applied. Allow ⅛-inch of wood around outside edge of caster. Made in ⅝, ¾ and ⅞ inch sizes. Made of hardened steel, heavily nickled.

Come-Packt Price, (all sizes per set of 4) **$0.10**

FREIGHT RATES IN CENTS PER 100 POUNDS

	A	B	C	D	E	F	G	H
	$1.16	$0.95	$0.95	$1.16	$1.16	$1.74	$2.32	$2.32
Ala., Mobile	1.16	.95	.95	1.16	1.16	1.74	2.32	2.32
Ark., Little Rock	1.20	1.20	.92	1.40	1.40	2.80	2.80	4.20
Ariz., Phoenix	2.60	2.60	2.20	3.00	3.00	6.00	6.00	9.00
Calif., Stockton, San Jose, Los Angeles, San Francisco, Sacramento	2.60	2.60	2.20	3.00	3.00	6.00	6.00	9.00
Colo., Denver, Pueblo	1.67	1.67	1.41	2.13	2.13	4.03	4.26	6.39
Conn., All Points	.70	.61	.61	.70	.70	1.05	1.40	2.10
Del., All Points	.63	.55	.55	.63	.63	.95	1.26	1.89
Dist. Col., All Points	.60	.52	.52	.60	.60	.90	1.20	1.80
Fla., Pensacola	1.16	.95	.95	1.16	1.16	1.74	2.32	2.32
Ga., Savannah	1.35	1.13	1.13	1.35	1.35	2.05	2.70	3.10
Idaho, Pocatello	2.46	2.40	2.13	2.86	2.86	5.49	5.72	8.58
Ill., Chicago	.37	.32	.32	.37	.37	.56	.74	1.11
Ill., Cairo	.50	.44	.44	.50	.50	.75	1.00	1.50
Ind., Indianapolis	.37	.32	.32	.37	.37	.56	.74	1.11
Iowa, Davenport	.55	.50	.55	.55	.55	.82	1.10	1.65
Kan., Leavenworth	.87	.80	.72	1.01	1.01	1.79	2.02	3.03
Ky., Louisville	.44	.37	.37	.44	.44	.66	.88	1.32
La., New Orleans, Baton Rouge	1.16	.95	.95	1.16	1.16	1.74	2.32	2.32
Me., Portland	.70	.61	.61	.70	.70	1.05	1.40	2.10
Md., All Points	.60	.52	.52	.60	.60	.90	1.20	1.80
Mass., All Points	.70	.61	.61	.70	.70	1.05	1.40	2.10
Mich., Detroit	.16	.14	.14	.16	.16	.24	.32	.48
" Grand Rapids	.30	.26	.26	.30	.30	.45	.60	.90
Minn., St. Paul, Duluth	.83	.70	.70	.83	.83	1.25	1.66	2.49
Miss. Natchez	1.16	.95	.95	1.16	1.16	1.74	2.32	2.32
Mo., St. Louis	.46	.40	.40	.46	.46	.69	.92	1.38
Mont., Butte, Helena, Anaconda	2.73	2.60	2.28	3.08	3.08	5.74	6.19	9.24
N. C., Wilmington	1.10	.95	.95	1.10	1.10	1.65	2.20	2.80
Neb., Omaha	.87	.80	.72	1.01	1.01	1.79	2.02	3.03
N. H., All Points	.70	.61	.61	.70	.70	1.05	1.40	2.10
N. D., Fargo	1.35	1.30	1.14	1.47	1.47	2.66	2.94	7.41
N. J., All Points	.63	.55	.55	.63	.63	.95	1.26	1.89
N. Y., Syracuse	.50	.45	.45	.50	.50	.75	1.00	1.50
N. Y., Buffalo	.41	.35	.35	.41	.41	.62	.82	1.23
N. Y., New York City	.63	.55	.55	.63	.63	.95	1.26	1.89
N. Mex., Deming	2.07	2.07	1.86	2.40	2.40	4.80	4.80	7.20
Nev., Reno	2.60	2.60	2.20	3.00	3.00	6.00	6.00	9.00
Ohio, Cincinnati	.39	.33	.33	.39	.39	.60	.80	1.17
Okla., El Reno, Oklahoma City	1.44	1.44	1.24	1.70	1.70	3.40	3.40	5.10
Ore., Portland, Astoria	2.60	2.60	2.20	3.00	3.00	6.00	6.00	9.00
Pa., Philadelphia	.61	.53	.53	.61	.61	.93	1.22	1.83
Pa., Pittsburgh	.41	.35	.35	.41	.41	.62	.84	1.23
R. I., All Points	.70	.61	.61	.70	.70	1.05	1.40	2.10
S. C., Charleston	1.00	.86	.86	1.00	1.00	1.50	2.00	3.00
S. D., Sioux Falls	.89	.83	.74	1.04	1.04	1.85	2.08	3.12
Tenn., Memphis	.91	.70	.70	.91	.91	1.37	1.82	1.82
Tex., Houston, Galveston, Dallas	1.60	1.60	1.31	1.87	1.87	3.74	3.74	5.61
Utah, Ogden, Salt Lake City	2.35	2.29	2.03	2.73	2.73	5.23	5.46	8.19
Vt., All Points	.70	.61	.61	.70	.70	1.05	1.40	2.10
Va., Richmond	.60	.52	.52	.60	.60	.90	1.20	1.80
W. Va., Wheeling	.41	.35	.35	.41	.41	.62	.84	1.23
Wash., Tacoma, Vancouver, Spokane, Seattle	2.60	2.60	2.20	3.00	3.00	6.00	6.00	9.00
Wis., Milwaukee	.43	.37	.37	.43	.43	.65	.86	1.29
Wyo., Cheyenne	1.67	1.67	1.41	2.13	2.13	4.03	4.26	6.39
Canada, Vancouver, B. C.	2.60	2.60	2.20	3.00	3.00	6.00	6.00	9.00
" Toronto	.41	.35	.35	.41	.41	.62	.84	1.23
" Montreal	.63	.55	.55	.63	.63	.95	1.26	1.89
" Halifax	.70	.61	.61	.70	.70	1.05	1.40	2.10
Mexico, City of Mexico, Torreon	2.26	2.26	2.10	2.26	3.58	4.12	4.12	5.96
" San Luis, Potosi, Monterrey	2.12	2.12	1.96	2.12	3.31	3.85	3.85	5.69
" Pachuca	2.22	2.22	2.06	2.22	3.51	4.05	4.05	5.89

SECTIONAL FURNITURE

A All chairs.
B All tables, (except dining tables and dressing tables). Sectional bookcases.
C Dining tables and porch swings.
D Davenports, settees, couches, costumers, umbrella stands, plant stands, sanitary desks, tabouretts, footstools, bookshelves, pedestals, phone stands.

ASSEMBLED FURNITURE

B Refrigerators.
E Bookcases, china closets, shoecabinets, cellaretts, shirtwaist boxes, music cabinets, cedar chests, hallchests, desks, dressers, chiffoniers, chifforobes, washstands, buffets, footstools, screens, clocks, hall mirrors, serving trays, lamps, fireless cookers, pianos, suction cleaners, mattresses, mirrors, sewing machines, rugs, carpets, linoleum, kitchen cabinets, dressing tables.
F Chairs, tables, (except dining tables and dressing tables).
G Settees, davenports, phonestands, plantstands, umbrella stands, costumers, bookshelves, bed springs.
H Willow furniture.

Duty to Canada—Thirty per cent ad valorem on all furniture, lamps and brass ornaments.

Duty to Mexico—Cushioned or upholstered furniture 30 cents per Kilo Mexican money. Other furniture twenty cents per Kilo Mexican money. Brass ornaments 50 cents per Kilo Mexican money. Lamps 70 cents Kilo Mexican money.

Duty to Australia—35 per cent ad valorem on all furniture.

Duty to Cuba—25 per cent ad valorem on all furniture.

Export Orders—Come-Packt furniture is specially adapted for export shipment and receives expert attention in our Foreign Department. Freight rates given to all points upon application. An extra charge of 5 per cent is made to cover packing charges on all export shipments routed via steamer. This does not apply to all rail shipments to Canada or Mexico. Export packing consists of extra heavy boxing, water proof paper lining, and steel taped edges. 20 per cent should be added to the weights for export boxing. On large shipments, we are able to save weight by packing a number of pieces in one box.

We agree to place goods f. o. b. (free on board) steamer New York City at a rate not to exceed $0.75 per 100 pounds (3 shilling) (4 francs) (3 marks) (4 lira.) Approximate cubic contents will be quoted on any list submitted.

Freight Rates—The above rates per Hundred Pounds apply on our Sectional Furniture from Ann Arbor or Toledo to points named. If your own city is not in the table, take the freight rate to the nearest point named and multiply it by the shipping weight (given under the description of each piece), and the result will be the approximate charge to your station.

The minimum freight charge is the least amount that Railroads accept for transporting freight to a given point regardless of its weight or classification. (See minimum charge column in rate table.)

The list in opposite column gives the classification of the different articles we are listing. For instance, if you live in Mobile, Ala., and you wish to get the freight charges on a sectional davenport to your city, the shipping weight will be found under the description of the piece, and by looking down the classification list you will see that the sectional davenports go under class "D", and in the freight rate table," "D" takes a rate of $1.16 per hundred pounds. In other words, if the shipping weight was 200 pounds, the total freight charge would be $2.32.

By referring to the group or classification letter, and the corresponding letter in the freight rate table, the rate may be obtained to various shipping points.

These freight rates were in effect on the date this catalog was published July 1st., 1912, and are subject to change by the Transportation Companies without notice. All delivered prices are quoted for immediate acceptance only.

NOTICE—The fore part of this catalog is devoted to our sectional furniture. In figuring up freight charges, be sure to notice whether the article in question is shipped in sections or only completely assembled. Case Goods, (buffets, dressers, etc.,) are shipped almost completely assembled as they are assembled in our factories in order to fit doors and drawers, and would take up approximately the same space if shipped K. D.

Dining room tables are never shipped assembled, nor are the bed davenports and sanitary desks. Assembled furniture is crated securely, but lightly as is consistent with safety.

Finishes and Cushion Materials

The Plates on the reverse side of this page* (specimens are one half actual size) reproduce the colors of our Mission Finishes and Cushion Materials as faithfully as is possible by color photography. We will gladly furnish actual specimens of our cushion materials and the finished wood on request.

Come-Packt Mission Finishes and Stains

Excepting the FUMED OAK, our Mission stains are deep penetrating, quick drying *spirit stains*. *They produce a brilliant, permanent color that will not fade, wear off, or raise the grain of the wood.* Where any stain will be exposed to the action of strong sun-light, a coat of shellac should be applied over it before polishing with wax. (COME-PACKT FURNITURE IS SHEL-LACED thoroughly before waxing). COME-PACKT finishes bring to full life the exquisite markings, or flakes, of the QUAR-TERED WHITE OAK which is used exclusively in our Sectional Furniture. These stains may be easily applied by an inexperienced person and produce beautiful effects on some of the less expensive woods that are commonly used for interior finishing work. 4 to 6 days should be allowed to complete these finishes.

Fumed Oak

The genuine ammonia process, (used exclusively by us), produces a chemical change in the wood by the action of the ammonia on the tannic acid of the oak,—the ammonia penetrates deeply into the fibres of the wood and a peculiar rich toned nut brown color results that is impossible to produce in any other way,—Red Oak cannot be successfully fumed. This process cannot be satisfactorily applied by inexperienced persons. 5 to 7 days should be allowed for this finish.

White Enamel

The best enamels are applied over maple, birch or other close grained hard woods. (Cheap, so-called, enamels usually consist of one or two coats of white lead paint on soft wood). Three to four under-coaters are put on and sanded down between each application, then from three to four coats of genuine enamel are applied and each coat is carefully sanded and the last two coats are hand rubbed and polished. This produces a finish that will endure and give perma-nent satisfaction. 21 days is a short allowance for this process, so we keep enameled pieces finished and ready for shipment. French Gray or other special finishes are made up to order only.

Varnish Finishes

Stains and fillers are applied to the wood before the varnish is put on. Each coat of varnish is lightly sanded to produce a smooth even surface and then the last two coats are rubbed with pumice stone and oil and a deep lustrous surface is obtained, or the process is continued until a very bright or polished surface results,—some-times called a piano polish. Fifteen to eighteen days is necessary for these finishes. Any of our Mission designs will be given a rubbed or polished finish at 10% net extra. Pieces will not be shipped in sections when given a rub or polished finish. Mahogany, Birch Mahogany and White Enamel are kept in stock completely finished.

Imperial Leathers

Our IMPERIAL leathers are the best and most carefully made imitation leathers obtainable. They are the best of a dozen or more grades and are far superior in wearing quality to anything but the grain hides which we use exclusively except where noted. The back-ing is a heavy sateen and the surface coating is hand buffed. We GUARANTEE our Imperial leathers to be satisfactory in point of service and appearance. A choice is offered between the large mark-ings or *Spanish* grain and the small or "NATURAL GRAIN".

Cowhide

Our COWHIDES are the best quality obtainable,—commer-cially known as the outside, or "grain" hides except where noted. We use these grain hides wherever our descriptions specify "cow-hide". Your choice of the "Smooth," or "Spanish grain".

D. B. Leather

The deep buff leather is a genuine cowhide in which a deeper buff has been taken off than in the leather above, and there is not quite so much of the grain showing,—this leather, however, is not to be confused with the cheap and unsatisfactory "middle" and "flesh" splits and where listed in descriptions of pieces it will wear and give lasting satisfaction. This grade is better than is ordinarily sold as the best genuine leather.

Roan Skin

Roan skins are IMPORTED GOAT HIDES, (sometimes called "Morocco leather") and are the finest, toughest and most durable upholstery leather obtainable, but on account of the small size of the hides, they cannot be used on some classes of work. The leather is remarkably soft and flexible and is tanned and dyed in beautifully brilliant colors. These skins are furnished in the "peb-bled grain" only.

Panne Mohair Plush

We use the finest grade of silk plush on a mohair backing. This covering is particularly suited to the genuine mahogany and birch mahogany pieces, it is stocked in the *dark red, steel blue, and tan only.*

Striped and Figured Denims

The denims make an excellent low priced covering for some of the larger pieces,—they will give good service and when worn out, may be easily replaced, if desired, with the more expensive fabrics like the panne plush or the genuine leathers.

Tapestry Cloth

There are so many grades, colors and kinds of genuine tapestry fabrics, varying in price from 50 cents to $8.00 a yard, that we have not attempted to carry them in stock. If you prefer a tapestry covering for any of the pieces you contemplate ordering, we will make a suitable reduction in our price and will use any covering material furnished by you. ALL MISSION DESIGNS IN THIS CATALOG REQUIRING CUSHIONSWILL BE UPHOLSTERED OVER AUTO-TYPE SPRINGS,—THE BEST, MOST COMFOR-TABLE AND MOST SATISFACTORY FLOATING SPRING CUSHION EVER MADE.

As an added convenience to our customers and not as an argument for economy, we will completely assemble our furniture and ship it ready for immediate use at a net extra cost of five per cent, which merely covers the added expense of wrapping and crating. We will gladly quote delivered prices on our furniture to any desti-nation, but please *do not ask for our discount sheet, as we have none,—our prices are the same to all regardless of the size of the order.* You pay no more and no less than your neighbor. Our prices are high enough to permit us to furnish the kind and quality of goods represented. Any reduction in price would necessitate a lowering in quality of materials, workmanship and finish. We would prefer to limit our output rather than lower the quality of the goods that have made the COME-PACKT name and Trade-Mark so justly famous.

Come-Packt Furniture Company
BEN RILEY, President and General Manager

*See inside back cover.